So What's the Deal with Love?

Joey O'Connor has worked in youth and family ministry for fifteen years in Southern California. He is a conference speaker and author of fourteen books for couples, parents, and young adults. He lives with his wife and four children in San Clemente, California, where he likes to surf, eat fish tacos, and lie in the hot sand.

His works include:

So What Does God Have to Do with Who I Am?

You're Grounded for Life & 49 Other Crazy Things Parents Say

Have Your Wedding Cake and Eat It Too: You Can Be Happy and Married

I Know You Love Me, But Do You Like Me? Becoming Your Mate's Best Friend

Women Are Always Right & Men Are Never Wrong

Heaven's Not a Crying Place: Teaching Your Child about Funerals, Death, & the Life Beyond

In His Steps: The Promise

Excuse Me! I'll Take My Piece of the Planet Now

Whadd'ya Gonna Do? 25 Steps for Getting a Life

Breaking Your Comfort Zones

Graffiti for Gen X Guys by J. David Schmidt with Joey O'Connor

Graffiti for Gen X Girls by J. David Schmidt with Joey O'Connor

For speaking events, conferences, and seminars, please call 1-877-447-4377. You can also write to Joey O'Connor at P.O. Box 3373, San Clemente, CA 92674-3373. Visit Joey's web site at http://www.joeyo.com. You can email Joey with your comments and questions at: joey@joeyo.com

So What's the Deal with Love?

Joey O'Connor

Fleming H. Revell
A Division of Baker Book House Co
Grand Rapids, Michigan 49516

© 2001 by Joey O'Connor

Published by Fleming H. Revell
a division of Baker Book House Company
P.O. Box 6287, Grand Rapids, MI 49516-6287

Printed in the United States of America

Library of Congress Cataloging-in-Publication Data

O'Connor, Joey, 1964–
    So what's the deal with love? / Joey O'Connor.
      p.   cm.
    ISBN 0-8007-5770-X
    1. Church work with teenagers. 2. Teenagers—Religious life—
Miscellanea. 3. Love—Religious aspects—Christianity. 4. Friendship—
Religious aspects—Christianity. 5. Sex—Religious aspects—Christianity. 6. Family—Religious aspects—Christianity. I. Title.
BV4447 .O245 2001
248.8'3—dc21   2001034953

For current information about all releases from Baker Book House, visit our web site:
                        http://www.bakerbooks.com

This book is dedicated to Jim Burns,
a true friend, mentor, and encourager.

I am forever grateful for your presence in my life.

"Greater love has no one than this,
that he lay down his life for his friends."
John 15:13

Contents

Introduction

So what's the deal with love?

That's a good question, and it's not a good question just because I'm the one asking it. It's a good question because you've probably asked yourself the same question long before you picked up this book. In fact, young people have been asking themselves and one another, "So what's the deal with love?" longer than you might imagine.

Think about it—long before Elvis was swinging his hips and proposing to his sixteen-year-old sweetheart, Priscilla, the King was wondering, "So what's the deal with love, PRA-SILLA baby?" And long before Shakespeare penned his famous love sonnet in junior high, "Ode to 7-Eleven Slurpees," you can bet he wondered, "So what art thy deal with love?" as he got pummeled at the bike racks for writing love notes to some babe named Juliet, who just so happened to be dating a guy in pink tights named Romeo. Though I'm no Elvis, Shakespeare, or Romeo, the first time I asked myself, "So what's the deal with love?" was when my first girlfriend, Christi Dial, dumped me like a bar of slippery soap on our one-month anniversary at the Valentine's Day dance in eighth grade. After her friends delivered the death-blow message for her, Christi was off chomping on pizza as though she had just chewed up my heart and spewed it all over the dance floor for other junior highers to stomp and slow dance on.

Everyone, and I mean everyone, asks the question, "So what's the deal with love?"

The only problem is that practically everyone you speak to has a different idea, definition, reason, recipe, or explanation of what love is or isn't. Love means a lot of different things to different people, and there are a lot of different types of love. You may love Slurpees at 7-Eleven, but that's different from how you love your dog. Your friend may say, "I love red Volkswagen Beetles," but you know it's quite difficult to develop an intimate, interpersonal relationship with a car that looks like a Skittle on four wheels.

Love for friends feels and looks different than love for family, which is different than love for nacho cheese Doritos, which is different than love for your favorite band, which is different than love like-oh-my-goodness-that-guy-over-there-is-so-cute-restrain-me-now-before-I-trip-and-fall-and-make-a-complete-idiot-over-myself, which is drastically different than loving corned beef on St. Paddy's Day, which even though I'm Irish, tastes absolutely loathsome, so on that point I'll stop and simply agree with Tina Turner, "What's love got to do with it?"

Since so many people have so many ideas, thoughts, and experiences about what love is or isn't, this book is going to take you straight to the source of true love. I am going to laser your attention on the One who loved you long before you ever heard the words, "I love you," and who loved you long before you ever

Introduction

received your first Valentine's Day card in kindergarten, though it was pretty cool getting a couple dozen cards filled with colored sweetheart candy in pink messages, "You're Awesome," "Be Mine," and "My True Love."

This is the deal with love: God loves you and has created you to enjoy him forever. He loved you before your parents, brothers, sisters, friends, boyfriends, or girlfriends, ever loved you. With so many people wondering what the deal with love is, couldn't we get to the heart of this question by going to the heart of God first? "This is love: not that we loved God, but that he loved us and sent his Son as an atoning sacrifice for our sins. Dear friends, since God so loved us, we also ought to love one another" (1 John 4:10–11). No matter who you are or what you've done, God loves you because he created you, and because he created you, you are very special to him.

In this book, you're going to discover what a radical difference God's love will make in your friendships, your family, your relationships with the opposite sex, and most importantly, in your relationship with God. Throughout this book you'll read all sorts of questions asked by teenagers who wonder what God's Word has to say about their specific struggles with parents, friends, dating, school, youth groups, peer pressure, temptation, grief, and all of the triumphs and troubles of growing up. We'll tackle tough topics like fighting with friends, loneliness, gossip, sexual choices, lust, temptation, obeying parents, and feeling unloved. When you read the Scripture verses, don't stop there. Grab a Bible and check it out for yourself. Still confused or got more questions? Talk to a Christian friend, youth pastor, your mom or dad, teacher, or someone who can steer you in the direction of God's love.

Introduction   11

So love really is a big deal, because once God's love gets hold of your life, it rattles you forever. You'll never be the same. God's love is such a big deal that after you read this book, you should pass it on to a friend who just might be wondering, "So what's the deal with love?"

Introduction

1

Friendly Fire

It happened in the Vietnam War. In the Panama Invasion. And in the Persian Gulf War too. *Friendly fire.* Getting shot at from the enemy is to be expected, but what about getting blasted by the people who are supposed to be on your own side?

There's a good chance you've been a victim or at least a target for friendly fire. In friendships it happens all the time: a bayonet in the back, verbal assaults, land mines packed with explosive lies, Stinger missile misunderstandings, hand-to-hand combat. You name it—friendships can be battle zones.

From the tensions caused by the need for acceptance to the confusion of trying to help a hurting friend, friendships aren't easy. Friendships take work, and good friendships take a lot of work. There's a fine art to choosing and keeping the right types of friends. Tragically, there are far more friendly fire fatalities than there are victories. The stories are as painful as they are endless.

I know a high school sophomore named Bob. If you asked me if Bob had friends, I'd say, "Yeah, he's got a lot of friends." But if you asked Bob, he'd tell you he doesn't have any. Bob's a nice guy, he plays on the tennis team and is involved in school and church activities. But in his mind, he still doesn't have any friends. Bob feels like he doesn't fit in. No matter how often I tell Bob that he does "fit" because of the many people that love him and care about him, Bob still feels like an outsider. Bob's not ugly, and he doesn't have unusually strong body odor, but he feels like no one understands him. What Bob really wants are good friends. Bob seems to know everyone on campus and in his youth group, but to Bob, no one knows him. Bob has stepped on the land mine of loneliness.

To Denise, acceptance by her friends is her life. What her friends and the important people on campus think of her is the single burning issue on her mind. Her parents are divorced, and her mom, with whom she lives, doesn't make much money, but Denise hangs out with friends whose parents have the bucks. Since she can't do much to raise her economic standard of living, Denise is working really hard (too hard) to raise her social standard of living. Running for class offices, meeting semi-important students who know very important upperclassmen, and checking out the party scene consume a lot of her time. In the battleground of friendship, Denise is working very hard to gain the acceptance of others.

Loneliness. Acceptance. Peer pressure. Tensions. Loyalty. One lonely guy and a girl just wanting to be accepted. Bob and Denise are only two examples of students wrestling with what it means to have a friend and what it means to be a friend.

Where is God when you've been hit by friendly fire? Whether you have a whole school full of friends or you've experienced

Friendly Fire

the shell shock of being blown to bits by friendly fire, be assured that God is interested in you and your friendships. He created friendships, and he is the very One who wants to develop a tight and lasting friendship with you.

God's Word offers all sorts of creative ways to deepen your friendships, how to choose and lose friends, how to handle the pressures of friendships, and how to know the difference between a good friend and someone who doesn't even know how to spell the word. Read on to discover the meaning of friendship from God's perspective and find his peace in the midst of friendly fire.

Friendship Battles
When You're in a Fight

Friends fight. Some fight dirty and some fight clean, but God understands that friends, even the best of friends, get into arguments, disagreements, squabbles, and fifteen-round knockout matches. When you're going at it with a friend, it's important to remember that what you do and say can permanently damage your friendship. The reasons for a fight or what actually happens in a fight aren't as important as what happens after the fight. God uses forgiveness, love, patience, and humility for mending and strengthening friendships.

My best friend lied to me; does Jesus understand the hurt I feel?

Even my close friend, whom I trusted, he who shared my bread, has lifted up his heel against me.

PSALM 41:9

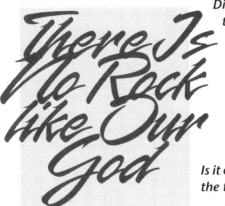

There Is No Rock like Our God

"Don't stop! Keep climbing . . . it's almost dark!" Todd's voice echoed up the granite rock face as I stood on a small ledge pulling up my rope, desperately looking up the rock for the next crack system to climb. Slung across my shoulder, my heavy rack of rock-climbing gear—carabiners, wire stoppers, camming devices, and belay rings—gently clinked and pinged like a metal wind chime as the night shadows blanketed the thousand-foot vertical face of Tahquitz Mountain. My Casio watch glowed 8:45 p.m. as I placed my next piece of gear into the vertical crack. That sucker had better hold, I thought to myself as I began my next series of moves. Lead climbing in the

(There's more!!)

I got into a fist fight with my best friend, and now he won't even speak to me. Did anything like that ever happen in the Bible?

If an enemy were insulting me, I could endure it; if a foe were raising himself against me, I could hide from him. But it is you, a man like myself, my companion, my close friend.

PSALM 55:12–13

Is it okay that my friends and I argue all the time?

Finally, all of you, live in harmony with one another; be sympathetic, love as brothers, be compassionate and humble.

1 PETER 3:8

I've been betrayed by a good friend; does Jesus understand?

Jesus replied, "Friend, do what you came for." Then the men stepped forward, seized Jesus and arrested him.

MATTHEW 26:50

Must I love a friend who hurt me?

If anyone says, "I love God," yet hates his brother, he is a liar. For anyone who does not love his brother, whom he has seen, cannot love God, whom he has not seen. And he has given us this command: Whoever loves God must also love his brother.

1 JOHN 4:20–21

Friendship Battles

dark, by myself, by Braille, and by starlight, wasn't my idea of how I wanted to spend my Saturday night.

Todd, Rich (my climbing partners a hundred feet below me), and I were on our way to spending a long, freezing cold night on a teeny ledge tied into a tiny tree. (You know, the same ledge and tree you've seen in hundreds of Wile E. Coyote cartoons!) That ledge was our home for the next nine hours because we were still a hundred feet from reaching the top, minus head-lamps, NeverReady flashlights, or Hollywood premiere searchlights lighting our way from the base of the mountain. We didn't have any food, water, fridge, TV, sleeping bags, microwave popcorn, or cellular phones to call home. (Yes, my wife, Krista, who was ONLY eight months pregnant with our first child would have appreciated a phone call!) And you thought you got into trouble for not calling home or being out past curfew?

Fortunately, our unplanned bivouac on the mountain never became the next episode of Rescue 911, and the only beating we took was from the hugs and slugs of family and friends when we arrived safely home the next day. Things could have been different if we hadn't had the essential ropes, har-nesses, climbing gear, and safety-minded climbing partners. Our night on the rock, however unplanned, didn't become the disaster it could have been mainly because we had the right type of gear.

Every year people die rock climbing because of three basic reasons: (1) not having the right type of gear; (2) not knowing how to use the right gear; and (3) attempting difficult climbs far beyond their experience. Land mine defusing, rocket testing, Brahma bull dancing, and rock climbing are not sports for fools. If you want to be a rock climber, you need not only the right type of gear but also adequate instruction.

Like rock climbing, life is dangerous, and if you want to survive the endless tests and temptations of being a teenager, like bagging your walk with God, having sex before marriage, trying drugs or alcohol, stealing, tagging, or join-ing a gang, you need the right equipment to give you a foothold above the crowd. For example, I've got a high school climbing buddy named Jake. Jake's crazy about God, and he's also crazy about climbing. Jake knows he could hang out with other climbers who want to party, but he's more inter-ested in pleasing God than drinking with someone who's holding the other end of his rope. Jake hangs out with good friends who are as solid as strong handholds and footholds. He's climbing through life with friends that pull him up instead of letting him fall.

You and I would be foolish to climb a thousand-foot rock face without a

(See page 18.)

rope; we'd also be crazy to take on life without God's Word. Jesus Christ said you can tell the difference between wise and foolish people by what type of foundation they build their life on. The same is true of rock climbers: Would you rather climb on granite or flaky sandstone that crumbles like brown sugar? The most solid rock you can build your life on is God's Word (see Matthew 7:24–27).

If you're a rock climber or you're interested in learning how to rock climb or you just want to keep climbing with Jesus, here are some great verses and tips to help you rope up with God. Staying tied into God and letting him lead your life is the most exciting adrenaline rush you'll ever experience.

CLIMBING TIP #1: KNOW YOUR CLIMBING PARTNER

"He is the Rock, his works are perfect, and all his ways are just. A faithful God who does no wrong, upright and just is he" (Deut. 32:4). Your life will never be in spiritual danger with God as your climbing partner. How often will you find a climbing partner who'll never make a mistake?

CLIMBING TIP #2: KNOW THE ROCK YOU'RE CLIMBING ON

"There is no one holy like the LORD; there is no one besides you;

(Check out the oval!!)

☞

I said some things I shouldn't have, and now I've ruined a good friendship. What can I do to restore it?

Repent, then, and turn to God, so that your sins may be wiped out, that times of refreshing may come from the Lord.

ACTS 3:19

I don't understand; why do friends sometimes say cruel things?

The tongue also is a fire, a world of evil among the parts of the body. It corrupts the whole person, sets the whole course of his life on fire, and is itself set on fire by hell . . . but no man can tame the tongue. It is a restless evil, full of deadly poison.

JAMES 3:6–8

I have a friend who keeps stabbing me in the back; am I supposed to keep forgiving her?

Then Peter came to Jesus and asked, "Lord, how many times shall I forgive my brother when he sins against me? Up to seven times?" Jesus answered, "I tell you, not seven times, but seventy-seven times."

MATTHEW 18:21–22

My best friend hurt me; is it okay that I'm holding a grudge against her?

Friendship Battles

there is no Rock like our God" (1 Sam. 2:2). This world is filled with tons of options, choices, and decisions. Even though you could choose to climb all sorts of routes and rocks, there never was, is, or will be a Rock like God. He's the rock you want to climb.

CLIMBING TIP #3: KNOW THE MOUNTAIN CONDITIONS

"Great is the LORD, and most worthy of praise, in the city of our God, his holy mountain" (Ps. 48:1). God wants you to be all that he is. Climbing on his mountain and growing in holiness like him is part of the Christian adventure.

CLIMBING TIP #4: KNOW YOUR PROTECTION IS SECURE

"He alone is my rock and my salvation; he is my fortress, I will never be shaken" (Ps. 62:2). Protection is helpful only when it works. Having

(One to go!!)

☞

Bear with each other and forgive whatever grievances you may have against one another. Forgive as the Lord forgave you.

COLOSSIANS 3:13

My friend keeps digging up issues and problems of the past that I can't change. Does it say somewhere that God doesn't remember our sins?

"I, even I, am he who blots out your transgressions, for my own sake, and remembers your sins no more."

ISAIAH 43:25

Friendship Frustrations
Struggles with Friends

Don't you hate it when some bozo in class drags his fingernails down the chalkboard? *Ssscrrreeeech!* Frustrations in friendships are a lot like that: They're often temporary, but they can make your spine wanna jump out of your back. Frustrations left unset-

God as a fortress, you may take a fall or two, but you'll never be shaken enough to stop climbing.

CLIMBING TIP #5: CLIMB A PERFECTLY SAFE ROUTE

"As for God, his way is perfect; the word of the LORD is flawless. He is a shield for all who take refuge in him" (Ps. 18:30). God's way is the perfect route you want to climb. Don't waste your time on routes that are dangerous and unprotected. Foolish people who flirt with death live short lives.

CLIMBING TIP #6: BEWARE OF LOOSE ROCK

"For their rock is not like our Rock" (Deut. 32:31). You can climb on sandstone if you want to die. You can climb on loose, avalanche-prone rocks if you want to go for a slide. There's a lot of loose rock in this world . . . beware of imitations!

CLIMBING TIP #7: ATTITUDE IS EVERYTHING

"May the words of my mouth and the meditation of my heart be pleasing in your sight, O LORD, my Rock and my Redeemer" (Ps. 19:14). Checking your attitude is the first step to pleasing God. In everything you do, watch your words and actions. Tongues are slippery when wet and can cause a lot of unnecessary falls.

CLIMBING TIP #8: REJOICE IN THE ROCK

"The LORD lives! Praise be to my Rock! Exalted be God, the Rock, my Savior!" (2 Sam. 22:47). We're not talking about moon or tree worship here . . . we're talking about living a life of praising God, the Rock of our salvation.

CLIMBING TIP #9: LET GOD DO THE LEADING

"Since you are my rock and my fortress, for the sake of your name lead and guide me" (Ps. 31:3). There's a bumper sticker you've probably seen—Lead, Follow, or Get out of the Way! Drop the first and last ideas. Just follow God and you'll be okay.

CLIMBING TIP #10: NEVER GIVE UP!

"With my God I can scale a wall" (Ps. 18:29). When you're climbing with God, you're climbing with the Creator of the universe! He can help you scale the biggest immovable, impossible wall you've ever faced! God made the rock; he can move it!

(Author's note: Rock climbing is an inherently dangerous sport and should never be attempted without proper instruction from a trained professional, like Bobo the rock-climbing clown.)

(That's all!!)

Friendship Frustrations

tled will continue to grate and grind on your nerves until you talk to your friend and deal with the problem. Here's some perspective on dealing with the tensions and troubles that come through friendships.

I have a Christian friend who's very selfish. How can I help him see that trying to be first is not always the best?

"But when you are invited, take the lowest place, so that when your host comes, he will say to you, 'Friend, move up to a better place.' Then you will be honored in the presence of all your fellow guests. For everyone who exalts himself will be humbled, and he who humbles himself will be exalted."

LUKE 14:10–11

Is it possible to find a friend who can keep a secret?

A gossip betrays a confidence, but a trustworthy man keeps a secret.

PROVERBS 11:13

How can I know God's peace in my struggles with my friends?

"I have told you these things, so that in me you may have peace. In this world you will have trouble. But take heart! I have overcome the world."

JOHN 16:33

The treasure of having a friend for life is a rare opportunity. And the discovery of a loyal friend is worth more than a pirate's bounty. Unfortunately, many friendships today aren't worth sailor spit. Here are five long-lost qualities you can develop to unlock the hidden world of lasting friendships. If you develop these qualities, it'll be no secret to those around you.

Realness. A friend who is real is the type of friend you can see through. They don't wear masks or try to be someone they aren't. Real people are open with their thoughts, struggles, frustrations, and dreams. A friend who is real isn't a squeaky-clean image of perfection but rather someone who can look in the mirror and laugh.

Risk-taker. A friend who takes risks isn't someone who challenges you to lick bare feet, wash car windows on the freeway, or drink alcohol concoctions that taste like jet fuel. A friend who takes risks is the

(Keep reading!)

☞

Friendship Frustrations

type of friend who will get in your face when you're blowing it. Risk-taking friends always look out for your best interests, not their own. If they look foolish so you can look good, that's a risk they're willing to take. A risk-taking friend trusts you with their deepest hurts and shares their most awesome dreams. A risk-taking friend recognizes that friendship is fragile and therefore guards it with care.

Responsible. A good friend is "response-able." When a problem comes up between the two of you, they don't blow up. Instead, they are *able* to make an appropriate *response*. Responsible friends have a growing understanding of what builds up (and blows up) friendships. A responsible friend understands the meaning of the word *consequence*—"for every action there is a reaction." A responsible friend has figured out what happens when you mix drinking and driving and understands the hormonal juices of X and Y chromosome bodies. A responsible friend has both the brains and guts to say "Yes" to the right things and "See ya" to the wrong things.

Reliable. "We all need somebody we can lean on!" Don't ask me to sing the song, but a reliable friend is someone you can lean on. Reliable friends are honest, dependable, trustworthy, and consistent. They aren't er—r—a—ti—c. They don't change from one mood to the next in a matter of seconds. A reliable friend is the type of friend you can count on. No matter how hard you lean on them, they'll still be standing when others have fallen flat on their face.

Recreation. Recreation (creative fun) is an overlooked secret in the wild world of friendship. Most friends wait for someone else to come up with Friday night plans, but a creative friend makes things happen. They aren't attached to the typical regurgitated weekend events like renting videos, cruising, or hanging out at the mall. Creative friends are fun to be around. They make old ideas into new ones and refuse to give in to boredom. Learning how to play and play hard is a great way to deepen a friendship and create memories that will last forever.

(That's all!)

My friend has little habits that really bug me. Should I say something or just let it go?

A man's wisdom gives him patience; it is to his glory to overlook an offense.

PROVERBS 19:11

I've discovered that a very good friend of mine has some deep problems he's been hiding from me. This could divide our friendship; what should I do?

Friendship Frustrations

A friend loves at all times, and a brother is born for adversity.

PROVERBS 17:17

I have trouble with my temper; will I lose my friends if I don't learn how to control it?

"In your anger do not sin": Do not let the sun go down while you are still angry, and do not give the devil a foothold.

EPHESIANS 4:26–27

Did Jesus' disciples ever experience tension in their friendship with one another?

When the ten heard about this, they became indignant with James and John.

MARK 10:41

I have two "best" friends, but among the three of us, it seems we're always fighting over each other; what should we do?

Conformity has a cost. And it ain't cheap. How much are you willing to pay? Conformity is kind of like the drug dealer on the street. The first few hits he gives you are free, but once you're hooked, it's going to cost. Conformity has all sorts of payment plans. Choose any one you like, but when you conform to what others want instead of what God wants, there's always a price. A BIG price.

CONFORMITY PAYMENT PLANS

Cash. Must pay immediately with everything you have on you. The party scene is a very common place where teenagers pay up front for acceptance and recognition. If you have to choose between taking a stand for what you believe or looking like a geek, it's a lot easier to join the party

(This is great! Read on!!)

☞

If you have any encouragement from being united with Christ, if any comfort from his love, if any fellowship with the Spirit, if any tenderness and compassion, then make my joy complete by being like-minded, having the same love, being one in spirit and purpose.

PHILIPPIANS 2:1–2

I have a friend who's very inconsiderate; he's always getting into my stuff, taking food out of the fridge, and never cleans up after himself. What should I do?

If your brother sins against you, go and show him his fault, just between the two of you. If he listens to you, you have won your brother over.

MATTHEW 18:15

Friendship with God
The Ultimate Friend

God is the ultimate friend. He will never let you down, never change, and never talk behind your back. His love for you is so strong that nothing can overcome it. You can completely be yourself when you're hanging out with God. He is the most loyal friend you'll ever have, but like a best friend, he's counting on you being loyal too. Check out what friendship with God is like through what he has to say to you in his Word.

How can I be sure that God will always be my friend?

The LORD appeared to us in the past, saying: "I have loved you with an everlasting love; I have drawn you with loving-kindness."

JEREMIAH 31:3

Since I can't see God, how can I be sure he's with me?

Friendship with God

"When you pass through the waters, I will be with you; and when you pass through the rivers, they will not sweep over you. When you walk through the fire, you will not be burned; the flames will not set you ablaze."

ISAIAH 43:2

Did God ever call anyone his friend?

And the scripture was fulfilled that says, "Abraham believed God, and it was credited to him as righteousness," and he was called God's friend.

JAMES 2:23

What is the true extent of God's love for me?

"Greater love has no one than this, that he lay down his life for his friends."

JOHN 15:13

I've heard that you're either God's friend or you're not; is that true?

You adulterous people, don't you know that friendship with the world is hatred toward God? Anyone who chooses to be a friend of the world becomes an enemy of God.

JAMES 4:4

Did Jesus ever call anyone his friend?

"I no longer call you servants, because a servant does not know his master's busi-

and be like everyone else. However, the more you party, the more difficult it is to leave when you discover how empty your wallet and your life have become.

Check. Students wanting to pay the cost of conformity by check must first have a current student I.D., two major credit cards, and no points on their driving record. Students who pay by check are actually paying cash, but it's just not as visible. Integrity issues like borrowing homework, going to two movies when you've paid for one, and stealing from stores in the mall are not noticeable price tags in the cost of conformity. But nonetheless, they accrue more debits than credits in God's account.

Thirty-Day Credit Plan. This "hidden" payment plan is often the one sexually active students bank on—"It could never happen to me!" "But we used birth control." The credit plan is simple: Your boyfriend convinces you that his love for you is lasting and sincere. So why not express your love for one another physically? Why not? Because the cost for premarital sex can be extraordinary (hospital bills, diapers, formula, clothes, etc.). But who can repair the hurt of hearing "I never loved you in the first place"? The Thirty-Day Credit Plan is enticing, but the payments can last a lifetime.

Plastic Payment Plan. Making payments by using

(One to go!!)

plastic is an arduous way to cover the cost of something you're now sick of. Those beers you began drinking a few years ago didn't look so bad then. The good friend you dumped in eighth grade because he didn't want to party is nowhere to be found now. Many students slap down the plastic to pay for experiences they can't afford in the first place. Nobody said conformity would cost this much.

Credit problems? Low on cash? Interest-free checking? God's got an incredible deal on grace . . . it's absolutely free! No money down, no layaway; you don't even have to have a nickel to your name. Grace is free! "For it is by grace you have been saved, through faith—and this not from yourselves, it is the gift of God—not by works, so that no one can boast" (Eph. 2:8–9).

(That's all!)

ness. Instead, I have called you friends, for everything that I learned from my Father I have made known to you."

JOHN 15:15

What does God expect from my friendship with him?

"You are my friends if you do what I command."

JOHN 15:14

How does God prove that he's my friend?

But God demonstrates his own love for us in this: While we were still sinners, Christ died for us.

ROMANS 5:8

Sometimes I'm not a very good friend to God; what should I do?

Then I acknowledged my sin to you and did not cover up my iniquity. I said, "I will confess my transgressions to the LORD"—and you forgave the guilt of my sin.

PSALM 32:5

How can I be sure God's friendship for me won't change no matter what I do?

Friendship with God

He who is the Glory of Israel does not lie or change his mind; for he is not a man, that he should change his mind.

1 SAMUEL 15:29

Being Lonely

A Land Mine Called Loneliness

Shut out? Loneliness can be compared to being on a deserted island by yourself. Wrong. Deserted islands still have water, coconuts, and little thatched huts you can sit under. If you've ever been lonely (even if you still have friends), then you know that loneliness is more like stepping on a land mine. If the loneliness you've experienced is like an antipersonnel mine, then it's just enough to wound you (like blowing your leg off), exposing enough sensitive nerves and causing you just enough pain to never want to get close to anybody again. God has a lot to say about loneliness. He understands your thoughts and feelings better than anyone else. He also wants you to know that his presence will help you even if you feel paralyzed and stuck in the middle of a minefield you never planned on entering.

As hard as I try, I just don't seem to fit in. How can I make friends?

"For I know the plans I have for you," declares the LORD, "plans to prosper you and not to harm you, plans to give you hope and a future."

JEREMIAH 29:11

I've recently moved away; how can I keep from being lonely?

Being Lonely

27

Fall Guy

Ever thought about becoming a stuntman or stuntwoman when you get out of school? Yeah, it could be pretty cool getting paid tons of cash for driving fast cars, diving out of exploding buildings, skateboarding under moving semitrailers, and punching out bad guys until they become bleeding, limp lumps of flesh. Not bad for a day's work, eh? Should you choose to accept this glamorous, bone-breaking, death-defying Hollyweird career, here's the best way NOT to begin. This story has warning labels pasted all over it. . . .

One night, when I was a junior in college, a group of guys and girls in a dorm close by were having a party. The scene was happening on the fourth floor, approximately forty to fifty feet above planet Earth. Alcohol was flowing like a faucet at full bore. The music was blaring. It was definitely Miller Time.

In the dorm room where the party was raging, there was a small patio deck that ran right

(Check out page 30!!)

☞

"No one will be able to stand up against you all the days of your life. As I was with Moses, so I will be with you; I will never leave you or forsake you."

JOSHUA 1:5

Did Jesus ever feel lonely?

About the ninth hour Jesus cried out in a loud voice, "Eloi, Eloi, lama sabachthani?"—which means, "My God, my God, why have you forsaken me?"

MATTHEW 27:46

How can I choose the right type of friends?

"But seek first his kingdom and his righteousness, and all these things will be given to you as well."

MATTHEW 6:33

I'm told the reason I don't have very many friends is because I'm too shy. Didn't God make me this way?

But now, this is what the LORD says— he who created you, O Jacob, he who formed you, O Israel: "Fear not, for I have redeemed you; I have called you by name; you are mine."

ISAIAH 43:1

Am I the only one who's ever been lonely?

Turn to me and be gracious to me, for I am lonely and afflicted. The troubles of my heart have multiplied; free me from my anguish.

PSALM 25:16–17

Being Lonely

I have a tendency to repel people; what can I do to become more lovable?

Be imitators of God, therefore, as dearly loved children and live a life of love, just as Christ loved us and gave himself up for us as a fragrant offering and sacrifice to God.

EPHESIANS 5:1–2

The friendships I develop are always good at first, but they never seem to last; how can I keep from getting discouraged?

We also rejoice in our sufferings, because we know that suffering produces perseverance; perseverance, character; and character, hope.

ROMANS 5:3–4

Being like Jesus

Loving the Unlovables

If you've ever been teased, ridiculed, or snubbed by others who thought they were better than you, then you know what it's like to feel unloved and unlovable. A lot of times that feeling is reinforced by parents who don't care, teachers who spot our weaknesses, and friends who think we're losers. I've got good news for you: God loves the unlovables. And if you think you're unlovable, God loves you all the more! Jesus Christ didn't come for the person with the highest GPA or best-looking body; he came for people who aren't perfect and know it. If you're a Christian and God has blessed you, you've got a mission: Love the unlovables.

I sit across from a real jerk in science class. This guy drives me crazy; does God expect me to actually love him?

alongside the red tile roof. On any given day, the guys who lived on the top floor of this dorm (stuntmen-in-training) would walk twenty or so feet on the roof from one patio deck to the next. Totally exposed. No air bag below. Fearless. (Okay, okay . . . *fearless* and *stupid* can be used interchangeably here.)

On this cold, wet Friday night, one of the party-goers, a definite stuntman-in-training, locked himself out of his room. No key, no problem. Have roof, will travel. Fortunately, his room was just next door to where the party was going on. He could walk right across the tile roof and onto his patio like he had done many times before. Luckily, all he had to do was pop open his window to let himself into his room. Unfortunately, his stomach was holding more beer than all of Germany during Octoberfest, and unluckily, the red tile roof was slippery slick from the dew of the night. You gettin' da picture here?

Our inebriated stuntman-in-training didn't get halfway across the roof before his feet began screaming, "Traction, traction . . . we need TRACTION!" Slipping. Twisting. Falling. This guy was not going to be late for his appointment with Mr. Gravity. His screams, drowned out by loud music, weren't even heard by his friends. About halfway down, somewhere between the twenty- and twenty-five-foot marker, a wrought-iron balcony—get this—*broke his fall* . . . as well as a few other important items like ribs and a jawbone. Unfortunately (again!), the balcony flubbed the catch of the plummeting collegian and allowed the unforgiving earth to swallow him whole. *Fwuumpp!*

(There's more!!)

☞

"The King will reply, 'I tell you the truth, whatever you did for one of the least of these brothers of mine, you did for me.'"

MATTHEW 25:40

My youth pastor talks about reaching out to students who don't have any friends. I know this is a good thing, but how do I do that?

Be wise in the way you act toward outsiders; make the most of every opportunity. Let your conversation be always full of grace, seasoned with salt, so that you may know how to answer everyone.

COLOSSIANS 4:5–6

I get tired of trying to be nice to people who don't have friends; it seems like they don't care about me. What should I do?

Being like Jesus

Let us not become weary in doing good, for at the proper time we will reap a harvest if we do not give up.

GALATIANS 6:9

How can I accept students who aren't very popular?

Live in harmony with one another. Do not be proud, but be willing to associate with people of low position. Do not be conceited.

ROMANS 12:16

Did Jesus face opposition for hanging out with undesirable people?

"The Son of Man came eating and drinking, and they say, 'Here is a glutton and a drunkard, a friend of tax collectors and "sinners." But wisdom is proved right by her actions.'"

MATTHEW 11:19

So many people on my campus don't have friends. Does God care about these people?

The LORD is close to the brokenhearted and saves those who are crushed in spirit.

PSALM 34:18

Will God help me develop a Christlike attitude toward needy people?

The Spirit of the Sovereign LORD is on me, because the LORD has anointed me to preach good news to the poor. He has sent

Our stumpman, I mean, stuntman, furiously met the hard ground with all the grace of an out-of-control dud missile. His head landed a mere two inches from a cement curb. Miraculously, this fall guy survived with only a few broken bones and a deeper appreciation for gravity, iron balconies, and extra room keys.

Been a fall guy lately? Messed up like an amateur stuntman with no business walking on slippery roofs? Blown it so bad that you know everyone is going to be talking about you at school on Monday? Fallen so far that you feel like you might as well write off those chances you had to get that date, go to that concert, borrow the car, have a starting position, or go away for the weekend with your friends? Taking a spill stinks, but purposely falling and meeting the natural consequences of our own bad decisions makes for a harsh landing.

Let's face it: I'm a fall guy. You're a fall guy. We're all fall guys. When it comes to sin and making bad choices, we're suckers for temptation and testing slippery surfaces. We'd like to think we shoot high, but sometimes our best aim is straight down to the balcony below us. We've all heard that "pride goes before a fall,"

(See page 33!!)
☞

me to bind up the brokenhearted, to proclaim freedom for the captives and release from darkness for the prisoners.

ISAIAH 61:1

It seems that so many students lack compassion these days. How can I develop compassion like Jesus has?

When he saw the crowds, he had compassion on them, because they were harassed and helpless, like sheep without a shepherd. Then he said to his disciples, "The harvest is plentiful but the workers are few. Ask the Lord of the harvest, therefore, to send out workers into his harvest field."

MATTHEW 9:36–38

How can I explain to a friend who got dumped by her boyfriend that God understands her loneliness?

He heals the brokenhearted and binds up their wounds.

PSALM 147:3

Taking a Stand
Putting Up with Peer Pressure

Be cool! Peer pressure is a lot like gravity: No matter how hard you try to jump away from it, it's always going to have a pull on you. Even if you don't give in to the 1001 faces and forms of peer pressure, it will still affect you and the decisions you make. God's Word has loads to say about who you hang out with and why. Why not take his advice and learn that God's way is the easy way (does that sound like Mom and Dad or what)? Peer pressure may pull you in different directions, but like a father pulling his child from

but nobody said anything about smacking balconies on the way down.

All of us fall short. You name it, and we can do it, lose it, break it, miss it, drop it, and forget it. Let's be really honest and admit that not only do we fall short and miss the mark when it comes to living a perfect life according to God's Word, we also slam on the brakes when God's Spirit is telling us to hit the accelerator. We throw curveballs instead of shooting straight with God. We go offline when he wants us online talking with him. We trade spending time with him for MTV or ESPN as if he were an insignificant, mediocre baseball card. We go for the slam dunk on our own power instead of setting up the alley-oop for him to score big on. Our pride gets in the way. We begin to think we'll never slip. Never fall.

Acting like a spiritual stuntperson is risky. Believe me, there is no future in sin, and according to Romans 6:23, "the wages of sin is death." *Talk about a*

hard landing. Though our failings and fallings lead to death, God is ready to give us the gift of eternal life through his Son, Jesus Christ. Instead of getting grounded by God, we get grace. Instead of our daily flaws being fatal, we receive the free gift of eternal life.

Okay, as you read this article, what are you going to do if there's a forty- to fifty-foot distance between you and God? If you've fallen hard this past week or so, here's the best way to settle the score: Go for grace. Confess your sin. Your failings. Your fallings. In Jesus Christ, God promises to forgive and free you. He won't rub your face in the ground. Each day, you receive a fresh start. Sin always has a hard landing, but God's grace can even catch you before, during, or after a fall. His gift of grace will help you keep your feet on level ground . . . and your body off a balcony.

(That's all!)

the danger of a hot stove. God's hand on your life is stronger than the tug and pull of peer pressure.

My friends are always trying to get me to cheat for them. What should I do?

Blessed is the man who does not walk in the counsel of the wicked or stand in the way of sinners or sit in the seat of mockers. But his delight is in the law of the LORD, and on his law he meditates day and night.

PSALM 1:1–2

I love my friends, but because I'm not into partying like they are, they don't call me on the weekends. What can I do?

How to Get in the Middle without Getting Clobbered

"Come on, get in the car; we're not gonna wait here forever so you can figure out if this is a good moral choice or not. It's only a small party . . . you can call from Kim's bedroom when we get there . . . it's no big deal," your best friend pleads while the three people in the backseat stare at you as if you were wearing a pink ballerina tutu. A small party. You've heard that one before.

This is the third time in a month that the plans have "suddenly changed." Your best friend's canned lines are becoming vaguely familiar:

If I had known earlier, I would've told you so.
Going to the drag race wasn't my idea; it was Pete's!
How was I supposed to know there was going to be booze at the party?
Listen . . . nobody forced you to come with us . . . you could have said no.

Your friend's life is going down the drain. Down the toilet. Right into a stinking sewer. You smell it. You feel it. You see it. You know it. It doesn't take a rocket scientist to figure out what a stupid decision looks like, but what do you do when your friend's one or two stupid decisions are now suddenly a lifestyle?

What are you supposed to do when the person you've hung out with the past few years doesn't like hanging out with you anymore? Okay, maybe she won't admit it, but you can tell she's real careful about what she says around you now. When you ask what she's doing this weekend, she: (1) avoids the subject; (2) says she hasn't decided yet, which means (a) she's lying, (b) she's keeping her options open, (c) she's blowing you off; (3) tells you she's already made plans with Tina and that automatically XXX's you out of the picture since your friend knows you won't hang out with Tina because you know what Tina's all about. How can you help

(Don't stop here!!)

Taking a Stand

The LORD is a refuge for the oppressed, a stronghold in times of trouble. Those who know your name will trust in you, for you, LORD, have never forsaken those who seek you.

PSALM 9:9–10

My friends are pressuring me to use drugs, and I'm scared; what should I do?

When I am afraid, I will trust in you. In God, whose word I praise, in God I trust; I will not be afraid. What can mortal man do to me?

PSALM 56:3–4

What can I do when I'm out shopping with my friends and they want me to shoplift?

Do not be misled: "Bad company corrupts good character."

1 CORINTHIANS 15:33

How do I choose between what my friends want and what my parents want?

Children, obey your parents in the Lord, for this is right. "Honor your father and mother"—which is the first commandment with a promise—"that it may go well with you and that you may enjoy long life on the earth."

EPHESIANS 6:1–3

I can't afford the clothes my friends wear; how can I fit in?

Therefore I tell you, do not worry about your life, what you will eat or

your friend see that she's blowing it? What can you do to win her back from her new "friends" who don't give a rip about her? How can you get in the middle without getting clobbered?

CONFRONTING YOUR FRIENDS

Dealing with friends who are doing dumb things is difficult. There's nothing easy about it . . . never has been . . . never will be. Half the crazy voices inside your gray-matter-filled-brain are taunting, "Oh, don't be such a wuss. She can make her own decisions; let her learn by her mistakes. Don't make such a big deal out of nothing." Your blood-pumping heart fights and screams back, "What are you thinking?

Don't just stand there . . . do something! Take a stand!"

If you're wrestling with deciding whether to confront your friend or not, here are some important questions to consider: What is the number one thing keeping you from facing your friend? I know it's a big risk to confront a friend, but staying silent can make things worse. God's Word can give you the strength and encouragement you need to confront your friends. Proverbs 27:19 says, "A mirror reflects a man's face, but

(There's more!!)

what he is really like is shown by the kind of friends he chooses" (NKJV). It takes a courageous friend to hold up a mirror and without being preachy, honestly say, "It's not a pretty reflection, but here's what your life looks like to me. I'm here to help you get cleaned up."

THE KISS OF DEATH

Jesus was betrayed with a kiss from someone who was supposed to be his friend. There are a lot of Judases today, and chances are they've infiltrated a few of your friendships. Your friends may not be sold for thirty pieces of silver, but stuff like drugs, alcohol, sex, stealing, cheating, and lying to parents are all like subtle, seductive, warm, tempting kisses. First your friend wants one . . . then another . . . then another. Before your friend knows it, she's a long way from Kansas, and Toto's nowhere in sight. Proverbs 27:6 says, "Wounds from a friend are better than kisses from an enemy" (NKJV). Are you a true friend or a Judas? Are you going to wound your friend or wimp out?

LAYING DOWN YOUR LIFE WITH LOVE

I can understand how you feel when it comes to talking to your friend. You may feel stupid, embarrassed, or not even sure of what you're going to say. In high school, I tried talking to a couple friends of mine tons of times, but all they did was blow me off. Jeff and Sean were partying all the time, not calling me, lying to me about what they did on the weekend, and in the end, our friendships disintegrated into nothing more than an occasional "hi" in the hallway at school. I felt stupid. I was often embarrassed about

(Check out page 37!!)

drink; or about your body, what you will wear. Is not life more important than food, and the body more important than clothes?

MATTHEW 6:25

Do I fit in with God?

The LORD will fulfill [his purpose] for me; your love, O LORD, endures forever—do not abandon the works of your hands.

PSALM 138:8

Is it okay that I feel envious of friends who are popular?

For where you have envy and selfish ambition, there you find disorder and every evil practice.

JAMES 3:16

Taking a Stand

Ever since I got my driver's license, my friends pressure me to drive as if I was in the Indy 500. What should I do?

A wise man fears the LORD and shuns evil, but a fool is hot-headed and reckless.

PROVERBS 14:16

Helping Friends

Reaching Out to Friends

Sharing your relationship with God with your friends may be one of the most difficult things you ever do. If you're like most students, you probably feel as if you don't know enough about God or the Bible or Jesus or even if you're really supposed to speak for God in the first place. At the same time, you also may know that Jesus placed a priority on making sure people heard his message. What to do? Remember that when you share with others what God means to you, it's he who starts, continues, and finishes his work in their lives. God wants you to be available, and he will enable you to do what he wants you to do. We are called to be the people of God before doing the work of God. The following verses will give you a good start in learning that.

bringing up topics they didn't want to talk about. Especially God. I lost a couple of good friends, but the most important thing I kept was my faith in Jesus Christ. I learned that even though I was willing to take the risk to talk to my friends about their negative choices, they were ultimately responsible for their lives. As a friend, I was responsible *to* them, but not *for* them.

The night Jesus was betrayed by Judas and deserted by his closest friends, he told them something I'm sure they never forgot, "The

(Don't stop now!!)

☞

Does praying for my friends matter to God?

Helping Friends   37

greatest love is shown when a person lays down his life for his friends" (John 15:13 NKJV). Even though Jesus' friends abandoned him, he still laid down his life for his friends. That's radical! When you put what you think and feel about talking to your friends aside and actually go and do what God wants you to do, that's when you're laying down your life for your friends. When you value your friends over your feelings of embarrassment, you are living out the sacrificial love of Jesus. That's laying down your life with love. And that's nothing to feel embarrassed about.

Ten Tips to Tackling Tough Talks with Friends

1. Don't preach . . . your friend needs a real friend, not a parent or a pastor. Maybe your youth pastor can help . . . why not ask?
2. Bring a friend. Maybe one or two other friends can help you out, but make sure everyone knows each other well.

(One to go!!)
☞

And pray in the Spirit on all occasions with all kinds of prayers and requests. With this in mind, be alert and always keep on praying for all the saints.

EPHESIANS 6:18

I've been praying for my friends, but I don't seem to see any change in their lives. What does God say about being persistent in prayer?

Pray continually.

1 THESSALONIANS 5:17

I have a friend who says Christians are just a bunch of hypocrites. How can I show her my faith is genuine?

Dear children, let us not love with words or tongue but with actions and in truth.

1 JOHN 3:18

How can I let my friend know that God can comfort him when he has problems?

Praise be to the God and Father of our Lord Jesus Christ, the Father of compassion and the God of all comfort, who comforts us in all our troubles, so that we can comfort those in any trouble with the comfort we ourselves have received from God.

2 CORINTHIANS 1:3–4

My friend says that Jesus is just one of "many" ways to get to heaven. What can I say to her?

Helping Friends

Jesus answered, "I am the way and the truth and the life. No one comes to the Father except through me."

JOHN 14:6

What can I say to a friend who thinks that God is out to condemn him?

"For God did not send his Son into the world to condemn the world, but to save the world through him."

JOHN 3:17

Should I be scared to share my faith with my friends for fear of being rejected?

"So don't be afraid; you are worth more than many sparrows. Whoever acknowledges me before men, I will also acknowledge him before my Father in heaven."

MATTHEW 10:31–32

How should I feel when my friends make fun of me for being a Christian?

"Blessed are those who are persecuted because of righteousness, for theirs is the kingdom of heaven. Blessed are you when people insult you, persecute you and falsely say all kinds of evil against you because of me. Rejoice and be glad, because great is your reward in heaven, for in the same way they persecuted the prophets who were before you."

MATTHEW 5:10–12

3. Start with an affirmation. Before you bite into the thick meat of the situation, serve up something easier to swallow, like how important the friendship is to you.
4. Make it clear that you're not condemning, just concerned.
5. Be specific. Don't refer to vague situations. Present clear facts that are based on truth, not rumor or exaggerations.
6. Avoid words like *always, never,* and *every;* they sound too extreme.
7. Find a place to meet that'll be free of distractions.
8. Be willing to own up to situations, conflicts, or inconsistencies about your own life that your friend may bring up. Honesty is a good bridge builder.
9. Focus on your feelings rather than your friend's failures. He's going to feel awkward enough without someone beating it into him.
10. Be ready to go the distance with your friend. Everything probably won't change in one meeting. Be willing to meet again and again. Pray for your friend and ask God to give you the wisdom you need!

(That's all!)

What can I say to a friend who says she has a hard time believing in someone she can't see?

We live by faith, not by sight.

2 CORINTHIANS 5:7

I have Christian friends who don't seem to care about sharing their faith; all they want to do is hang around other Christians. What should I do?

Preach the Word; be prepared in season and out of season; correct, rebuke and encourage—with great patience and careful instruction.

2 TIMOTHY 4:2

Taming the Tongue
Word Power

"Say that word again and I'll wash your mouth out with soap!" Our parents knew the power of the tongue, and by now, you've probably blown a few soap bubbles of your own. Nobody needs to tell you that words can build or destroy. Your words open the door to your heart. And when that door is left hanging open, everyone can look inside and see who you really are. Taming the tongue is learning when to slam the door shut. God wants his Word to leave a lasting impression on our lives. These verses will help you tame your tongue so that you can leave a lasting good impression on the lives of others.

What does God have to say about having a foul mouth?

Nor should there be obscenity, foolish talk or coarse joking, which are out of place, but rather thanksgiving.

EPHESIANS 5:4

I have a problem with gossip. What does God think?

40　　　　　　　　　　　　　　　*Taming the Tongue*

If anyone considers himself religious and yet does not keep a tight rein on his tongue, he deceives himself and his religion is worthless.

JAMES 1:26

The guys I hang out with are always bragging about their sexual exploits. How should I react?

Do not let any unwholesome talk come out of your mouths, but only what is helpful for building others up according to their needs, that it may benefit those who listen.

EPHESIANS 4:29

A friend is spreading rumors about me. What should I do?

Brothers, if someone is caught in a sin, you who are spiritual should restore him gently. But watch yourself, or you also may be tempted.

GALATIANS 6:1

My best friend accuses me of lying to him. This is the same guy I pray for . . . what can I do?

In return for my friendship they accuse me, but I am a man of prayer.

PSALM 109:4

My friends are always ripping on other people; how can I keep from being a part of it?

Have nothing to do with the fruitless deeds of darkness, but rather expose them.

EPHESIANS 5:11

Taming the Tongue

How to Lose a friend

This may sound crazy, but I want to help you lose a friend. Possibly more than one. Answer this one question: Are your friends pulling you up or dragging you down? If they're pulling you up, then you're a winner and you've got what other kids are dying for. But if your friends are pulling you down, then you're . . . oh, how could I best put this?

- On a sinking ship
- Playing Spin the Bottle in bathing suits
- Standing under a dying elephant
- Going down a paddle without a river
- Playing with dynamite
- Lighting the fuse of your dynamite
- Playing Russian roulette with a leaky squirtgun
- In deep yogurt

In the long run, losing friends who are pulling you down isn't that much of a loss. For some kids, I know it may take a few heartaches, a couple car accidents, maybe an arrest or two to convince them of that, because friendships are important. But what's more important than friendship is life. If your friends aren't enhancing the quality of your life (or maybe you're not helping much either), then it's time to seriously evaluate the friendship. It's not easy to say good-bye to a friend, but if you think it's time to let go and move on to healthier, positive friendships, here are some creative ways to say *adios, ciao,* and bye-bye:

- Move (send no forwarding address).
- Write a letter. Let them know how you feel.
- Play Paper, Rock, Scissors to see who goes to a different school.
- Politely decline invitations to parties.
- Study on weekends.
- Let them know that *you* have decided to make some changes.
- Place a "Most Wanted" picture of yourself in the post office and say you have to unexpectedly get outta town.
- Tell them that your parents won't let you see them anymore.
- Shave your head, refuse to shower, and chant, "Snodgrass, snodgrass."
- Tell your friend the truth. (This friendship isn't working.)

(That's all!)

Taming the Tongue

My best friend is telling everyone something I told her in confidence. How should I treat her?

Be kind and compassionate to one another, forgiving each other, just as in Christ God forgave you.

EPHESIANS 4:32

A couple girls in my class are always gossiping. I'm sick of listening to them; what should I do?

He who guards his mouth and his tongue keeps himself from calamity.

PROVERBS 21:23

Some of my friends lie without even thinking about it. How does God want me to respond when I'm tempted to lie?

Whoever of you loves life and desires to see many good days, keep your tongue from evil and your lips from speaking lies.

PSALM 34:12–13

Developing True Friendships

Real Friends

Let's face it: True friendships are not easily found or made. A lot of people are more interested in themselves than their friends, and when it comes to making personal sacrifices, a true friend is a rare find. Maybe that's why it's so difficult to develop lasting friendships. True friendships involve risk-taking, realness, and being brave enough to get in a friend's face when he's messing up. God took an incredible risk when he demonstrated his friendship to you and me by sending his Son, Jesus, into the world. Jesus offers his friendship to us daily, and by his example, he shows us what it takes to be a true friend. These verses

Later, Dude

Doesn't it bug you when you waste seven bucks on a dumb movie you thought was supposed to be an action/adventure blockbuster hit? Or what about when you're really psyched about the new person you're dating but after only two weeks they dump you? What's up with that? What a waste of time!

You can waste your hard-earned cash on a lame movie, but you don't want to waste your time on "friends" who pull you down instead of up. They're not friends at all; they're leeching losers. I'm not talking about friends who occasionally mess up (because we all, at one time or another, mess up!). I'm talking about real losers—people who incessantly tempt, challenge, and tease you to smoke, drink, steal, cheat, or lie. If you're hanging out with people like these, then you're either wasting your time or well on your way to becoming a USDA Choice Beef, Prime Cut Loser.

This world has two types of places for human garbage: dumps and cemeteries. Dumps are filled with trash, broken appliances, toys, rotten food, and stuff that's no longer needed. Cemeteries are filled with people who, in some cases, wasted their lives hanging out with the wrong crowd. That's a little harsh, you say? Oh yeah? Cemeteries are filled with teenage guys and girls whose famous last words were, "It'll never happen to me." "I can handle what I drink." "Who needs a seat belt?" "I'm a good influence on my friends . . . I can help them change." Do these lines sound a little too familiar? Who are you hanging out with? Are you wasting your time trying to impress a group of people who couldn't care less about you? Would you be willing to follow them into battle? Would they be willing to lay down their lives for you? Would you really be willing to lay down your life for them?

So how can you really know whether to lose a bunch of losers or not? If you're wondering whether you're wasting your time living with losers for friends, here are four specific ways the Bible weeds out the winners from the losers:

(Keep reading!!)

Developing True Friendships

will challenge you to be the type of friend that others would risk their lives for.

How should I react when a friend confronts me with some personal issues I need to work on?

Wounds from a friend can be trusted, but an enemy multiplies kisses.

PROVERBS 27:6

What does the Bible say about being a trustworthy friend?

A gossip betrays a confidence, but a trustworthy man keeps a secret.

PROVERBS 11:13

I need to ask a good friend for advice, but I'm not sure if I should.

1. "A friend loves at all times" (Prov. 17:17). We're not talking about a sappy, huggy-kissy type of love here but the kind of love that's solid, strong, and committed to your best interests. This is God's vice-versa type of love for friends; it goes both ways.
2. "Wounds from a friend can be trusted" (Prov. 27:6). A good friend will get in your face when you're blowing it. Losers will never tell you the truth about yourself 'cause they're in it for themselves. A good friend will bump you when you're outta line and do what it takes to keep you in line. A loser will never toe the line for you!
3. "If one falls down, his friend can help him up" (Eccles. 4:10).

Friends pull each other up. Losers knock each other down. Loser friends are often jealous, hyper-competitive, mean, and selfish. The type of friends you want will encourage you, strengthen you, support you, and help you to be the person God has designed you to be.
4. "The greatest love is shown when a person lays down his life for his friends" (John 15:13 NKJV). Are you hanging out with losers who don't want to change their lifestyle in exchange for God's lifestyle? There comes a critical point in time when nothing you say or do will change a loser's

(There's one more!!)

☞

attitude or actions; that's when you need to say "Later, dude" and find the type of friends who are worth dying for. If you're wondering whether to lose a loser or not, consider the ultimate friend who laid down his life for you. Jesus Christ is the most radical friend you'll ever have. He loves you at all times. He can totally be trusted. He'll pick you up when you fall, and he's already laid down his life for you. You'll never be wasting your time building a stronger friendship with Jesus. Just ask me— a former loser who finally listened to God.

(That's all!)

Perfume and incense bring joy to the heart, and the pleasantness of one's friend springs from his earnest counsel.

PROVERBS 27:9

I have a friend who's struggling, and it seems no one wants to help him out. How can I be a loyal friend?

If one falls down, his friend can help him up. But pity the man who falls and has no one to help him up!

ECCLESIASTES 4:10

How can I help a friend who's depressed all the time?

And we urge you, brothers, warn those who are idle, encourage the timid, help the weak, be patient with everyone.

1 THESSALONIANS 5:14

I have a friend who's in serious trouble; what can I do to help?

Is any one of you in trouble? He should pray.

JAMES 5:13A

Is it a good idea for my friends and I to commit our friendships to God?

Jonathan said to David, "Go in peace, for we have sworn friendship with each other in the name of the LORD, saying, 'The

Developing True Friendships

LORD is witness between you and me, and between your descendants and my descendants forever.'"

1 SAMUEL 20:42

What characterizes a really good friendship?

A man of many companions may come to ruin, but there is a friend who sticks closer than a brother.

PROVERBS 18:24

What does it mean to be a dependable friend?

Do not forsake your friend and the friend of your father.

PROVERBS 27:10

Is there any connection between being humble and being a good friend?

"But when you are invited, take the lowest place, so that when your host comes, he will say to you, 'Friend, move up to a better place.' Then you will be honored in the presence of all your fellow guests."

LUKE 14:10

Kick-Starting Friendship

Fanning the Flames of Friendship

Gotta love 'em!

There are times in your friendships when things seem flat, common, almost boring. Nothing will spark the fire of your friendships like encouragement. Encouragement sends the roots of your friendships deeper and deeper into the soil of significant and lasting relationships. A high five, a card in the mail, a crazy message left on an answering machine, or an "I Love You" written on the dirt of their windshield are just a few ways to encourage your friends. God's Word encourages us to be encouragers, people who reflect the God who believes in them.

Are You a trustworthy friend?

Are you looking for a trustworthy friend? Someone you can count on, tell secrets that will stay secrets, and who makes you feel like you can be yourself around them? Before looking any further, there are a lot of other people who are looking for those same qualities in you. Take this *Trustworthy Test* to see if you are the type of friend others are looking for.

Scoring Scale: To answer these questions, score yourself based on how trustworthy you are as a friend. *Answer the questions according to who you are as a friend, not according to who you'd like to be.* (All questions must be answered with a Dixon Ticonderoga pencil 1388-#2.) Place your name and period number in the upper right-hand corner.

Point Ranking
1. Sorry, this ain't friendship
2. Report to principal's office
3. Multiple unexcused absences
4. Lacking in motivation
5. Satisfactory
6. Room for improvement
7. A friend worth having
8. Looking real good
9. You're doing great
10. Everyone needs a friend like you!

Rank yourself. Circle the number that best describes what kind of friend you are.

(Be brave! See the next page!!)

Kick-Starting Friendship

1. Do you ever lie to your friends? 1 2 3 4 5 6 7 8 9 10
2. If you hear a rumor about a good friend of yours, do you automatically believe it or do you try to find out the truth by talking to your friend? 1 2 3 4 5 6 7 8 9 10
3. Can you keep a secret? 1 2 3 4 5 6 7 8 9 10
4. Can you keep a really juicy secret that you're dying to tell others? (It's poised on your tongue like a jet ready to be launched off an aircraft carrier!) 1 2 3 4 5 6 7 8 9 10
5. When your friend is going to make a decision that can threaten their safety or even their life and makes you swear to tell no one, do you? (Hint: A very good friend is interested in preserving life before anything else.) 1 2 3 4 5 6 7 8 9 10
6. Your friend won't pass their History final if you don't help them study this weekend. You promise to help, but then another friend invites you to go skiing. Do you go? 1 2 3 4 5 6 7 8 9 10
7. When your friend asks you to go out for the evening, are you usually late? 1 2 3 4 5 6 7 8 9 10
8. If you're going to be late meeting a friend or can't make a meeting, do you call? 1 2 3 4 5 6 7 8 9 10
9. Do you take risks with your friends by sharing your struggles and feelings? 1 2 3 4 5 6 7 8 9 10
10. Would others say you're trustworthy? 1 2 3 4 5 6 7 8 9 10

How Trustworthy Are You? Add up your score and see how trustworthy you are as a friend. If you scored high, way to go! If you didn't, remember that there's always room for improvement and this test is a good way to evaluate what you need to work on as a friend.

10–20 Points SEE "HOW TO HAVE A FRIEND FOR LIFE." You need help!

21–40 Points Can't spell the word. Could possibly end up making license plates in San Quentin someday. Should not be left in a room alone with cash, small children, or matches. A friend who loses friends very quickly.

41–60 Points You're the type of friend who has to apologize a lot. You could be a scatterbrain or just plain selfish. You'd have trustworthy potential if you'd realize that some friends will dump friends who continually let them down. You're not out of the game yet, but you've got a couple strikes against you. Hang in there! There is a God who believes in you and can help you become a better friend.

(Finish this up on page 50!!)

🖝

61–80 Points You're a team player, and you put your friends high on the priority list. You may blow it here and there, but you admit your mistakes and are willing to work things out. You aren't flaky or unreliable, and most of the time you know when to keep your mouth shut. There are probably a few areas you need to develop to strengthen your friendships, but you're definitely on the right track.

81–100 Points A lot of people could use a friend like you. You value honesty, trust, openness, and risk-taking. You know when to open your ear and when to keep your trap shut. Loyalty is important to you, and you consistently make good choices when it comes to your friendships. You scored so high, perhaps you should be writing this section instead of me? (You're the pro!) Hang in there being a great friend and be on the lookout for someone who doesn't have any friends.

(That's all!)

Is it possible to encourage a friend who's frustrated with trying to live a Christian life?

Consider it pure joy, my brothers, whenever you face trials of many kinds, because you know that the testing of your faith develops perseverance. Perseverance must finish its work so that you may be mature and complete, not lacking anything.

JAMES 1:2–4

I have a friend who just became a Christian; what does the Bible say about his decision?

"I tell you that in the same way there will be more rejoicing in heaven over one sinner who repents than over ninety-nine righteous persons who do not need to repent."

LUKE 15:7

What verse will encourage my friends in our weekly Bible study?

Kick-Starting Friendship

May the God who gives endurance and encouragement give you a spirit of unity among yourselves as you follow Christ Jesus, so that with one heart and mouth you may glorify the God and Father of our Lord Jesus Christ.

ROMANS 15:5–6

What can I say to a friend who feels like she has no direction for her life?

Let the morning bring me word of your unfailing love, for I have put my trust in you. Show me the way I should go, for to you I lift up my soul.

PSALM 143:8

I have a friend who's lazy about coming to church. How can I get her interested in going?

Let us not give up meeting together, as some are in the habit of doing, but let us encourage one another—and all the more as you see the Day approaching.

HEBREWS 10:25

How can my Christian friends and I make a stand for Christ in everything we do?

"By this all men will know that you are my disciples, if you love one another."

JOHN 13:35

Where do I find direction in being a good friend?

Teach me to do your will, for you are my God; may your good Spirit lead me on level ground.

PSALM 143:10

Kick-Starting Friendship

Sex: God's Body Language
Sex: God's Body Language
Sex: God's Body Language
Sex: God's Body Language
Sex: God's Body Language
Sex: God's Body Language
Sex: God's Body Language
Sex: God's Body Language
Sex: God's Body Language
Sex: God's Body Language
Sex: God's Body Language
Sex: God's Body Language
Sex: God's Body Language
Sex: God's Body Language

2

Sex: God's Body Language

Body. Cuerpuo. Corpus. Shintsai. Kah-RAH-dah. No matter what language you speak or what country you come from, God wants your body. It doesn't matter if you're a high school prom queen or a skinny freshman with a pimple the size of Everest between your eyes: God wants your body. Pretty weird concept, huh?

You see, your body was created by God, therefore the ownership is really his. But as a gift, he's handed it over to you to use. Actually, your body is both a gift and a loan, because you'll have to turn it in whenever God asks for it back. If you want to be all that God wants you to be in life, the best thing to do is give your body back to him so you can experience all the wonderful plans and purposes he has created for you.

Some people act as if their body is all theirs and not God's. They behave as if they'll never have to turn in their bodies or give an account to God for what they did with their bodies while here on earth; that's called rebellion, and rebellion is the language of sin. God says "Yes" and we say "No." We say "Yes" and God says "No." God doesn't speak this language, so communication becomes impossible, and we never get to hear what's on God's mind about what to do with our bodies.

Fortunately, God has given us his Word, the Bible, to communicate a very clear message about what to do with our bodies and why. God doesn't want us to just use and abuse our bodies, he wants us to give him our bodies as an act of worship. Giving God your body is one of the most important things you can do because God's Son, Jesus Christ, gave his body to be crucified so that we might have life through him. If God has you and your body, you'll experience the best God has to offer. You'll be able to experience his language of love for your life.

All this talk about bodies is meaningless unless we talk about sex. Not only is God interested in your body, he's concerned about your sexual decisions. He knows that the sexual decisions you make today will affect the rest of your life. God wants you to have a long and satisfying life (that includes a satisfying sex life), but that depends on you and the sexual decisions you make. You can honor God with your body by making positive sexual decisions. God created you and all the hormones that run rampant through your body. The one person he wants you to experience a satisfying and meaningful sexual relationship with is the person you marry. Being sexually active before mar-

Sex: God's Body Language

riage is the kind of decision God wants you to avoid, not because he's prudish, unjust, or unfair, but because he knows about the hurt and damage that result from relationships outside his design for marriage.

Too many young people today experience unnecessary pain from broken relationships, going too far too soon, or not knowing when to tell a boyfriend or girlfriend, "STOP!" God knows that your body can seem like it's going out of control, but just when you think you can't control yourself, he will give you the strength to make the type of choice that says, "Sorry, you can't have my body. It isn't mine. I gave it to God." Giving your body to God is not only a great way to show your love for God but also a way to experience his blessings as a result of your obedience. He wants your body, not so he can control you but so he can free you to be all that he wants you to be in Christ Jesus. God's Word has a lot to say about your sexual decisions. This chapter will help you better understand God's language of love concerning your sexuality.

Sex: God's Body Language

Sexual Choices
How Far Is Too Far?

Back up! The burning question in dating relationships today for many Christian young people is, "How far is too far?" This is a very honest, important, and relevant question for young people who are interested in pleasing God. It's also a very dangerous question because once you've figured out "how far is too far" in your physical relationship with your boyfriend or girlfriend, there's always the pull of your sexual feelings to go *just a little farther.* The Bible won't tell you how far is too far for every situation you are involved in; however, it does give specific guidelines for honoring God and the person you care about. Instead of just thinking, "How far can I go with my boyfriend or girlfriend in our sexual relationship?" you may want to ask yourself, "How can I honor God in my dating relationships?"

I just lost my virginity, and I feel awful. Will God forgive me?

"I, even I, am he who blots out your transgressions, for my own sake, and remembers your sins no more."

ISAIAH 43:25

Why is it important to wait to be sexually active until I'm married?

Marriage should be honored by all, and the marriage bed kept pure, for God will judge the adulterer and all the sexually immoral.

HEBREWS 13:4

Sexual Choices

Shut Up!

The other day while I was sweating and pumping to fight the flab on the Stairmaster at Family Fatness Center, I overheard a very peculiar conversation. Normally (I don't know if it's really normal), these high-tech workout centers are filled with spandexed, glistening bodies bulging with too-pumped-up-muscles attempting-to-be-greater-than-ARNOLD-held-together-by-panty-hose-material-four-sizes-too-small-and-dangerous-to-health-if-worn-too-long. It is amazing what the human body can do to get into clothes.

Anyway, while I was dying on the Stairmaster, right next to me were two junior high girls pumping away, going nowhere, like me. Eavesdropping on their conversation, I couldn't believe what I was hearing: "My thighs. I love the Stairmaster for my thighs. I can't stand the fat on my thighs." "Oh yeah, me too. The Stairmaster is sooo good for my legs too." Excuse me? Fat? Large thighs? These girls were not even mildly overweight. They were two cute girls trapped in the illusion that somehow their bodies were not good enough, skinny enough, or pretty enough. I thought to myself, *They don't need Stairmaster; they need a reality check.* I wanted to stop my workout, tap them on the shoulder, and say, "Excuse me, but I overheard what you two were talking about, and I thoroughly disagree with you. Neither of you is fat. And you don't

have large thighs. I think you both look great just the way you are." I didn't say anything. I was too chicken.

What you and I say can have a powerful effect on others. Hearing those girls talk about their "less than average" bodies, I wondered, *Did some guy say something to make them believe they're fat?* A crude remark. A gross joke. The tongue is a killer weapon, able to rip people up and down like a razor blade laced with acid. That slithery, wily, wet hunk of spit-covered muscle can be far more dangerous than any muscle-bound meathead with hams for arms.

Hanging out at the gym, I see all sorts of people very different than myself. Because they're different, weird thoughts and negative questions chase through my mind like a treadmill out of control. Call it self-preservation or just knowing when to keep still, at times my mind can barely restrain the negative words my tongue wants to spew out: *Excuse me, ma'am; did you jump off the lockers to get into that outfit? Sir, are those muscles real or do you take steroids?* Critical, cutting words reveal our own wimpy weaknesses. Not the weaknesses of others.

Do you have a problem keeping your mouth shut? Are you the type of person who tries to impress others by being quick

(Don't stop now!!)

☞

I'm so hungry for affection I let guys take advantage of me; is that wrong?

Each of you should learn to control his own body in a way that is holy and honorable, not in passionate lust like the heathen, who do not know God; and that in this matter no one should wrong his brother or take advantage of him. The Lord will punish men for all such sins, as we have already told you and warned you.

1 THESSALONIANS 4:4–6

How can I tell the difference between God's standards and the world's standards?

Do not deceive yourselves. If any one of you thinks he is wise by the standards of this age, he should become a "fool" so that he may become wise.

1 CORINTHIANS 3:18

My girlfriend and I are sexually active; should we make some changes?

Do you not know that your body is a temple of the Holy Spirit, who is in you, whom you have received from God? You are not your own; you were bought at a price. Therefore honor God with your body.

1 CORINTHIANS 6:19–20

Will God forgive me for making wrong sexual choices?

My dear children, I write this to you so that you will not sin. But if anybody does sin, we have one who speaks to the Father in our defense—Jesus Christ, the Righteous One. He is

---

with your tongue but slow with your mind? When you're playing hoops with friends, do you say, "Great shot" or "Great shot; did you play on the women's team?" Sitting in class, do you write gross notes to the guy everyone can't stand and then sign someone else's name? (Writing words = saying words = same thing.) Or at home, when your sister or brother takes the remote control, do you scream, "Listen, you idiot! Give it back before I rip your eyes out and throw 'em down the drain"? Or perhaps something less violent but equally damaging.

Raging forest fires. Tiny rudders that steer huge ships. Throat-burning poison. Bitter-tasting salt water. God isn't a lightweight in describing the power of the tongue. James (the guy who wrote the book named after him) spent a lot of time hanging out with Jesus. Jesus' influence on his life must have been pretty strong to have him write, "All kinds of animals, birds, reptiles and creatures of the sea are being

(A little more!!)
☞

Sexual Choices

tamed and have been tamed by
man, but no man can tame the tongue. It is a
restless evil, full of deadly poison. With the tongue we
praise our Lord and Father, and with it we curse men, who
have been made in God's likeness. Out of the same mouth come
praise and cursing. My brothers, this should not be" (James 3:7–10). The
words of James are heavy. He is serious about the tongue's muscle power.
Praising God and cursing people made in his likeness are not in God's fitness
program for spiritual growth.

Are you ready to let God help you get your tongue in shape? James said that no
man can tame the tongue, but we have a heavenly Father who is more than able to
help us tame what we cannot. Instead of being known as a wise-cracking-cheap-shoot-
ing-foulmouthed-poison-spitting individual with trash can lids for lips, how about being
a guy or girl who honors God by encouraging, affirming, praising, high-fiving, and
laughing with others made in his image? Your words can change others' lives. Tell
people the positive qualities you see in them. Speak softly instead of screaming.
Praise others when they do something good. Keep quiet instead of cussing. And
when all else fails and that slithery, forklike tongue slides out to squirt its
deadly poison, pull out the snakebite repellent that never fails: PRAYER.
Prayer is the heart muscle that can jerk the tongue into shape.

(That's all!)

the atoning sacrifice for our sins, and not only for ours but
also for the sins of the whole world.

1 JOHN 2:1–2

*My boyfriend and I are making sexual decisions that can have
severe consequences. How can we please God in our relationship?*

In the same way, count yourselves dead to sin but alive to
God in Christ Jesus. Therefore do not let sin reign in your mortal body so that you obey its evil desires.

ROMANS 6:11–12

Does the Bible say that only sexual intercourse is wrong?

"You have heard that it was said, 'Do not commit adultery.' But I tell you that anyone who looks at a woman lustfully has already committed adultery with her in his heart."

MATTHEW 5:27–28

What's the "bottom line" for making sexual decisions?

Love the LORD your God with all your heart and with all your soul and with all your strength. These commandments that I give you today are to be upon your hearts.

DEUTERONOMY 6:5–6

Dating Struggles
The Dating Dilemma

Dating is a dilemma. You get asked out by the guy you don't like, and your friend gets asked out by the guy you do like. Your date says she's starving, orders an expensive dinner, and then nibbles at it like a bird. The guy who picks you up is either too early, too late, or wearing enough cologne to send your family running for gas masks. Sometimes you don't know what to say or all your date talks about is himself. In fact, dating is such a dilemma, you've even considered writing a documentary on the subject for the Discovery Channel.

The pressure to date and the pressure of not having a date can be overwhelming. But did you know that the majority of high school students never have their first date until they're out of high school? Dating can be difficult, but it can also be a lot of fun as you get to know someone better and discover what you like in a person or don't. God wants you to develop healthy, positive friendships with members of the opposite sex. Even though the word dating may not be used in the Bible, God's Word has lots to say about developing good relationships.

I asked a girl out for a date and got rejected. Will God reject me too?

Praise be to God, who has not rejected my prayer or withheld his love from me!

PSALM 66:20

I didn't get asked to the prom. Doesn't God realize how important this event was to me?

Those who know your name will trust in you, for you, LORD, have never forsaken those who seek you.

PSALM 9:10

I've wanted to break up with my boyfriend for a long time, but I'm afraid to. What should I do?

"Be strong and courageous. Do not be afraid or terrified because of them, for the LORD your God goes with you; he will never leave you nor forsake you."

DEUTERONOMY 31:6

How can I please God in my dating relationships?

May he strengthen your hearts so that you will be blameless and holy in the presence of our God and Father

The Lust Buster

Controlling Your Thought Life Before It Controls You

Lust, that seemingly uncontrollable desire to possess something that isn't yours, can haunt, frustrate, break, pursue, and tear down the Christlike character God wants to develop in you. When you see a beautiful person, lust doesn't have to consume your every thought or wildest fantasy. God promises, "No temptation has seized you except what is common to man. And God is faithful; he will not let you be tempted beyond what you can bear. But when you are tempted, he will also provide a way out so that you can stand up under it" (1 Cor. 10:13).

God says he will give you a way out when you feel trapped by your thoughts, but the best way to a healthy thought life is to train your mind to be like Christ's. Paul wrote

(Check out the list on page 62!!)

to Timothy, a young man who faced temptation just like you, "Train yourself to be godly. For physical training is of some value, but godliness has value for all things, holding promise for both the present life and the life to come" (1 Tim. 4:7–8). Good training and knowing your escape route to God when you see trouble coming will help you live a life of purity and obedience. Looking for a few more ways? Some of these lust buster ideas may help you; okay, even if they're stupid, at least they'll get your mind off lust.

- Do your homework
- Cancel your cable TV subscription
- Roll in the snow
- Avoid walking in locker rooms of the opposite sex
- Take a cold shower after rolling in the snow
- Find a friend who can hold you accountable, pray with you, and support you
- Look the other way
- Throw away any pornography in your home or on your computer
- Rent *Bambi Thrashes Godzilla* instead of *Teen Babes in Babylon*
- Pray (read that again)
- Avoid Internet porn sites
- Write a letter to a friend
- Take up a new sport like bungee jumping, bronco riding, or shark fishing
- See what God's Word has to say about love, lust, sex, and thought life
- Become a vegetarian cave dweller
- Hang out with friends who pull you up instead of down
- Take down those questionable posters from your bedroom wall
- Use your binoculars for birdwatching instead of girl or guy watching
- Buy a pair of horse blinders
- Talk with your youth pastor
- Read 2 Timothy 2:22
- When all else fails, create your own list of Lust Busters

(That's all!)

when our Lord Jesus comes with all his holy ones. Finally, brothers, we instructed you how to live in order to please God, as in fact you are living. Now we ask you and urge you in the Lord Jesus to do this more and more.

1 THESSALONIANS 3:13; 4:1

I constantly need a boyfriend to cover up my insecurities. How can I find my security in God?

Finally, be strong in the Lord and in his mighty power.

EPHESIANS 6:10

Dating Struggles

There's a girl I really like and want to date, but she's not a Christian. What should I do?

Be wise in the way you act toward outsiders; make the most of every opportunity. Let your conversation be always full of grace, seasoned with salt, so that you may know how to answer everyone.

COLOSSIANS 4:5–6

What can I do when my friend spends time with her boyfriend and not with me?

Cast your cares on the LORD and he will sustain you; he will never let the righteous fall.

PSALM 55:22

How should I react when the girl I'm dating is becoming very possessive?

Above all else, guard your heart, for it is the wellspring of life.

PROVERBS 4:23

Advice from Parents

Parental Guidance Recommended

Don't you wish you had cool parents who would let you do anything you want? Do you ever wonder if your parents will ever stop being so overprotective? Why can't they just grow up? However old-fashioned, out of it, or just plain ignorant your parents are, God's Word places maximum respect on obeying, yes obeying, your folks. You see, you may think your parents are dumb, but God doesn't. He used *them* to bring *you* into this world, and he knows that even though parents make mistakes, they can help you avoid a lot of heartache by showing you how to make good choices. Dating is just one of the areas in which your parents might help you make good decisions.

Jesus Unplugged

Aborted attempt to be cool #3857429-1A. "Bulldozer" is the nickname of a studly jock adored and admired by all the girls on your campus. Possessing rippling, vein-popping, bulging biceps the size of gargantuan country fair watermelons, Bulldozer is a physiological wonder. But, as you and all the other guys on campus know, the real reason chicks dig him is because of his crewcut. Sporting nontoxic-water-based-mousse-styling-gel-usually-worn-by-women, Bulldozer is cool because he can do amazing things with his hair. Passing him at his locker, giggling, gorgeous girls love to run their fingers through his tight, spring-coiled spikes of hair. Snapping back to immediate attention, Bulldozer and his hair remain unfazed . . . chicks dig him . . . he knows it . . . that's cool. Bulldozer never has a bad hair day.

You figure that Bulldozer hasn't cornered the market on COOL. You can't bench press two lunch tables packed with cheerleaders, but you're ready to compete in the crewcut arena. Your best friend borrows his dad's 1957 Ward Cleaver–era buzz saw razor kit complete with assorted head-shearing attachments. Humming electric razor in hand and looking very nervous, your friend warns you that the last time this thing was used was when his dad tried to give the family dog a haircut. A day later, the dog ran away.

"I'm not kidding," your friend warns as he absolves himself of any responsibility for possible damages, "this thing's got a life of its own."

Twenty minutes later, you've got three bleeding head wounds. Hair blankets the floor. Stomach acid churns in your gnawing stomach. "MAYDAY!! MAYDAY!!" Something has tragically gone wrong. Doubled over on the kitchen floor and laughing hysterically, your friend screams, "You don't look like Bulldozer, you look like a pink shaved poodle!"

As in all emergency situations, you remain calm. "All it needs is a little mousse and it'll look fine," you half-heartedly defend yourself. Three handfuls of styling gel later . . . 2.8 minutes of brushing, primping, and flipping . . . the verdict is in: Your sheet-white, mole-speckled head looks and smells like an environmental waste hazard.

"Don't stand near any open flames," your ex-best-friend howls. He begs for an ambulance to take him away. You're ready to drive him away in a hearse. *This is NOT cool!*

(Next page, please!!)

Advice from Parents

(Parental Guidance Comic Relief Idea #4,874: Imagine your folks on their very first date. Recreate the comedy and romance of this momentous occasion on a videotape and give it to them for their anniversary.)

Why do my parents constantly lecture me about who I date?

Listen to advice and accept instruction, and in the end you will be wise.

PROVERBS 19:20

How can I keep from getting angry when my parents make me come home earlier from dates than my brother?

A fool gives full vent to his anger, but a wise man keeps himself under control.

PROVERBS 29:11

My parents embarrass me whenever my girlfriend is over. What can I tell my parents to make them stop?

Fathers, do not embitter your children, or they will become discouraged.

COLOSSIANS 3:21

My parents are old-fashioned; they refuse to let me date before I'm sixteen. Do I have to listen to them?

Listen to your father, who gave you life, and do not despise your mother when she is old.

PROVERBS 23:22

Every day, you face the challenge of being cool, keeping cool, and staying cool. If it's not the latest haircut, it's high-tops. If not hightops, it's hockey. If not hockey, then it's hanging out with the right people. To be cool today, the pressure is on to keep up with the latest movies, maga-zines, music, or models (the Cindy Craw-ford type . . . not F-16 airplane models!).

Not only can keeping up with cool be hazardous to your hair, keeping up with cool can be dangerous to your spiritual health. You see, there's a big difference between what this world *thinks* is cool and what God *knows* is cool. Jesus' disciples thought they knew a lot about being cool. That's when Jesus started to unplug every-thing the world had taught them.

James and John, Mr.-Oh-Too-Scary-Sons-of-Thunder-Dressed-by-Their-Momma-Boyz wanted to be cool by sitting at Jesus' right and left. Simon, Mr.-Tough-Guy-Bully-on-the-Synagogue-Corner-Zealot tried to be cool by fighting his way into God's king-dom. Peter, Mr.-Open-Mouth-Insert-Foot-Does-Not-Have-a-Clue-about-Being-Cool never knew when to keep his mouth shut.

(More cool stuff on page 66!!)

Matthew, Mr.-Thief-and-Traitor-Steal-from-the-Poor-and-Give-It-to-Mr.-Rich-Big-Man-Caesar-in-Rome had a very uncool reputation among his fellow Jews. Thomas, Mr.-Know-It-All-I-Won't-Believe-It-Unless-I-See-It-Man faced the triple-dog-dare of placing his hand and fingers into Jesus' hands and side. The Scriptures don't lie—Jesus hung out with a bunch of guys who weren't cool. The disciples were poor fishermen, thieves, social outcasts, and rebels. And that's what's so cool about Jesus. Jesus defines *cool* as serving instead of sitting. Making peace

(One more!!)

☞

My mom, who is single, is more concerned about her love life than me. Does God even care?

"Can a mother forget the baby at her breast and have no compassion on the child she has borne? Though she may forget, I will not forget you!"

ISAIAH 49:15

I want to date someone who isn't a Christian, but my parents won't let me. What should I do?

Children, obey your parents in everything, for this pleases the Lord.

COLOSSIANS 3:20

My parents never talk to me about sex. I have a lot of questions, so should I ask someone else? What should I do?

If any of you lacks wisdom, he should ask God, who gives generously to all without finding fault, and it will be given to him.

JAMES 1:5

Inner Beauty

Beauty from the Inside Out

Sweet!

Beauty isn't all it's cracked up to be. Try telling that to someone who's been disfigured with cystic acne or has been in a horrible car accident. In our society, beauty is important and beauty sells. It'll buy and get you dates. If you've been born with it, it's absolutely free, and with a little care, it'll last almost three-fourths of a lifetime.

instead of overpowering others. Giving instead of stealing. Speaking truth instead of lies. Trusting instead of doubting. Loving instead of hating. Jesus unplugs what you and I think cool is by living a lifestyle of cool. According to Jesus, real coolness comes from the inside, from the heart. Not from the outside, from crewcut hairdos.

God's Word says that Jesus didn't look cool, dress cool, or have good looks. He was a poor carpenter, and he didn't try to impress anyone: "But in our eyes there was no attractiveness at all, nothing to make us want him. We despised and rejected him—a man of sorrows, acquainted with bitterest grief. We turned our backs on him and looked the other way when he went by. He was despised and we didn't care" (Isa. 53:2–3 NKJV).

What makes Jesus cool? Even when we don't care about Jesus, he still cares about us. When we turn our backs on him, he doesn't turn his back on us. For guys desperate to be cool, Jesus is humble enough to show us what lasting cool is really all about. Get plugged into cool . . . plug into Jesus.

(That's all!)

Although too much importance is placed on outward, physical beauty, the real gem most people miss is inner beauty. You see, while the mirror may not be lying about what you look like on the outside, that's just a mere reflection of who God has created you to be. God is more interested in how beautiful you are on the inside than how you look compared to a mannequin or magazine cover. You are precious and special to God no matter how you look because God does not look at beauty like we do. He wants you to reflect the wonder of his beauty and not the mere image of outer beauty. God sees beauty from the inside out.

I secretly despise the popular "beautiful" people at school. What does the Bible say about that?

A heart at peace gives life to the body, but envy rots the bones.

PROVERBS 14:30

Am I any less important than others because I don't look as good?

As for those who seemed to be important—whatever they were makes no difference to me; God does not judge by external appearance.

GALATIANS 2:6

Is it okay for me to wish I was stronger and had better muscles?

My flesh and my heart may fail, but God is the strength of my heart and my portion forever.

PSALM 73:26

I know I'm not as attractive as most people my age. Can Jesus relate?

He grew up before him like a tender shoot, and like a root out of dry ground. He had no beauty or majesty to attract us to him, nothing in his appearance that we should desire him. He was despised and rejected by men, a man of sorrows, and familiar with suffering. Like one from whom men hide their faces he was despised, and we esteemed him not.

ISAIAH 53:2–3

I feel like I can never measure up to the people in movies and magazines. What should I do?

But now, this is what the LORD says—he who created you, O Jacob, he who formed you, O Israel: "Fear not, for I have redeemed you; I have summoned you by name; you are mine."

ISAIAH 43:1

My friends are caught up in their clothes, makeup, and hairstyles. How can I help them not place so much importance on these things?

Inner Beauty

"Therefore I tell you, do not worry about your life, what you will eat or drink; or about your body, what you will wear. Is not life more important than food, and the body more important than clothes?"

MATTHEW 6:25

I'm not very beautiful on the outside. What can I do to develop inner beauty?

Charm is deceptive, and beauty is fleeting; but a woman who fears the LORD is to be praised.

PROVERBS 31:30

Real Love

The Love Connection

Didn't an old patriot once say, "Give me love or give me death"? My brain synapses don't connect too often, but that's even more common when people talk about love. The brain and the emotions usually don't have much in common when it comes to love. One is interested in logic; the other, PASSION. God has wired you with a heart that is capable of giving and receiving love. The only problem is that there's so much confusion over what true love is and what it isn't. To plug you into the right connection so you can best understand what true love is, God's Word gives a specific look at the life of Jesus Christ. Jesus describes God's outpouring of love for a lost and hurting world. That's a connection you won't want to miss in the people you care about.

I wonder; what is real love all about?

This is love: not that we loved God, but that he loved us and sent his Son as an atoning sacrifice for our sins.

1 JOHN 4:10

True Love Checklist

How do you know if a guy or girl really loves you? How can you be sure they are interested in you as a person and not as an object, toy, possession, thing, or prize? The best definition of what true love is all about can be found in God's love letter to you and me: the Bible. Before you start doing back flips over someone you think you're in love with, make sure they have certain qualities.

Read 1 Corinthians 13 and then answer these questions.

- Love is patient. Is this person easily upset? What are they like when things go wrong? Can they endure fingernails scraping on a chalkboard?
- Love is kind. What do other people say about this person? Are they cruel? Are they considerate of you and others? Do they gossip? Are they known as kind to others?

(Read on!!)

I want to tell if a guy really loves me. How will I know?

Do nothing out of selfish ambition or vain conceit, but in humility consider others better than yourselves.

PHILIPPIANS 2:3

What's the difference between love and infatuation?

Love is patient, love is kind. It does not envy, it does not boast, it is not proud. It is not rude, it is not self-seeking, it is not easily angered, it keeps no record of wrongs.

1 CORINTHIANS 13:4–5

Is there a difference between God's love and human love?

Dear friends, let us love one another, for love comes from God. Everyone who loves has been born of God and knows God. Whoever does not love does not know God, because God is love.

1 JOHN 4:7–8

Love can be both powerful and mysterious; does the Bible talk about that?

Place me like a seal over your heart, like a seal on your arm; for love is as strong as death, its jealousy unyielding as the grave. It burns like blazing fire, like a mighty flame.

SONG OF SONGS 8:6

Real Love

How can I learn to love others as God loves them?

This is how we know that we love the children of God: by loving God and carrying out his commands.

1 JOHN 5:2

I want my love life to be filled with romance, passion, and mystery. Is this an unreal expectation?

Therefore do not be foolish, but understand what the Lord's will is.

EPHESIANS 5:17

What is the connection between God's love and Jesus Christ?

But God demonstrates his own love for us in this: While we were still sinners, Christ died for us.

ROMANS 5:8

If I love my girlfriend, why can't I express my love physically?

But among you there must not be even a hint of sexual immorality, or of any kind of impurity, or of greed, because these are improper for God's holy people.

EPHESIANS 5:3

- Love does not envy. How jealous does this person get? Do they get mad if you talk to other people? Are they too possessive or clingy?
- Love does not boast. Does this person brag a lot? Are they interested in you? Do they live for God's glory or their own glory? Is their ego in control?
- Love is not proud. Can this person admit their faults? Do they always have to get the last word? Can they compromise or do they always have to win?
- Love is not rude. Does this person's belching make you retch? Do they pick their nose in public? Do they make gross remarks all the time?
- Love is not self-seeking. Is this person selfish or selfless? Are they authentically interested in what's best for you? Do they put others before themselves?

(Keep reading on page 73!!)

☞

My feelings seem to take control of my love life; how can I let God help me?

> Search me, O God, and know my heart; test me and know my anxious thoughts.
>
> PSALM 139:23

Personal Purity

Making Purity a Priority

You live in a world obsessed with sexuality. Sex is in the movies and on TV, the Internet, and talk radio. Make no mistake about it, sex sells. Yet if you're a Christian, you serve a God who is holy. That means pure, one who is without sin. Because God loves us so much and wants the absolute best for our lives, he wants us to lead pure lives so we can reflect his holiness. Developing a pure heart, watching what goes in our minds, what we see with our eyes, speak with our mouths, and touch with our hands, are all priority decisions for our God who desires that we become like him. God created sex to be pure and holy. Your sexuality is a precious gift from God, and he wants you to enjoy it as he created it to be. A big step in growing closer to God is making purity a priority in your life. Why? "Blessed are the pure in heart, for they will see God" (Matt. 5:8).

Is sex bad?

> So God created man in his own image, in the image of God he created him; male and female he created them. . . . God saw all that he had made, and it was very good.
>
> GENESIS 1:27, 31

I've earned a reputation on campus for being "easy"; what can I do to change that?

Put to death, therefore, whatever belongs to your earthly nature: sexual immorality, impurity, lust, evil desires and greed, which is idolatry.

COLOSSIANS 3:5

Why is it so important for me to be obedient in the area of personal purity?

Make every effort to live in peace with all men and to be holy; without holiness no one will see the Lord.

HEBREWS 12:14

What does God have to say about personal purity?

Flee the evil desires of youth, and pursue righteousness, faith, love and peace, along with those who call on the Lord out of a pure heart.

2 TIMOTHY 2:22

How can I keep my focus on God in a world so focused on sex?

Let us fix our eyes on Jesus, the author and perfecter of our faith, who for the joy set before him endured the cross, scorning its shame, and sat down at the right hand of the throne of God.

HEBREWS 12:2

- Love is not easily angered. How short is this person's fuse? Do they get out of control in arguments? Do they leave holes in walls? Slam doors? Kick cats?
- Love keeps no record of wrongs. Does this person refer to past fights? When you say, "I'm sorry," are you forgiven? Do they talk about your faults but not their own?
- Love does not delight in evil. Does this person hate evil or is he or she indifferent to it? Are they a lover of what is good? Are they compassionate and caring? Are they sinister?
- Love rejoices with the truth. Is this person a liar? Do they have a reputation for not telling the truth? Do they hide secrets? Would others say they are honest?
- Love always protects. If the two of you were robbed, would this person give up their wallet or use you for a shield? Does this person give you a sense of security?
- Love always trusts. Can you share secrets with this person without fearing they'll tell everyone else? Are they dependable? Have they ever been indicted for fraud?
- Love always hopes. Is this person optimistic or pessimistic? Do they have confidence in their relationship with God? How do they handle adversity?
- Love always perseveres. Does this person face or run from

(One to go!!)
☞

problems? Can they handle conflict in a relationship? Have they ever run a marathon race?

- Love never fails. Is this person a quitter? Are they crushed by failure or do they try to learn something from it? Have they ever successfully defused a hand grenade?

(That's all!)

What is God's will for my body?

Therefore, I urge you, brothers, in view of God's mercy, to offer your bodies as living sacrifices, holy and pleasing to God—this is your spiritual act of worship. Do not conform any longer to the pattern of this world, but be transformed by the renewing of your mind. Then you will be able to test and approve what God's will is—his good, pleasing and perfect will.

ROMANS 12:1–2

What do God's holiness and my sexual decisions have in common?

It is God's will that you should be sanctified: that you should avoid sexual immorality.

1 THESSALONIANS 4:3

I know many Christians who are sexually active. Why shouldn't I be like them?

The righteousness of the upright delivers them, but the unfaithful are trapped by evil desires.

PROVERBS 11:6

Will God honor my desire to be pure like him?

"Blessed are the pure in heart, for they will see God."

MATTHEW 5:8

How can I live a pure life?

And this is my prayer: that your love may abound more and more in knowledge and depth of insight, so that you may be able to discern what is best and may be pure and blameless until the day of Christ.

PHILIPPIANS 1:9–10

Personal Purity

I get so discouraged trying to be pure like God wants me to; how can I trust in him to help me?

Everyone who has this hope in him purifies himself, just as he is pure.

1 JOHN 3:3

Living without Lust
Mental Madness

Lust . . . *guilt.* Dirty thoughts . . . *guilt.* Unreal fantasies . . . *guilt.* It's a horrible cycle, and it's a very common frustration for most young people (and many adults too). Imagine gathering all your friends and family in a movie theater to watch your favorite flick. Everyone's settled in, munching on their popcorn, when suddenly, instead of your movie, the hidden thoughts and dreams of your mind are flashed upon the screen. Would your secret thought life be the length of a feature film? Or would you have to give out season passes so they could finish watching it later? Lust is mental madness. It takes something that God created as good and reduces it to a selfish, possessive act. If you've struggled or are struggling with your thought life, there is hope. We serve a God who is forgiving and patient. He is able to help you with any problem, no matter how large or how crazy it makes you. You can have control over your thought life because God will not let you be tempted beyond what you can handle (see 1 Corinthians 10:13). Instead of trying to win the battle over your mind by yourself, give it to the God who is mad about you. Find a friend you can talk to. There's always strength in numbers.

How can I stop feeling guilty about my sexual thoughts?

This then is how we know that we belong to the truth, and how we set our hearts at rest in his presence whenever our

Generic Love Letter

Since you are so in love that you've begun to drool, lose all bodily control, and be blinded by the sheer radiance of your new amore, this generic love letter has been especially created for you. If you can't put two words together to make a coherent sentence, all you need to do is circle the word of your choice and send this palpitating piece of pure poetic passion.

(Mi Amore, Dude, My Love, Dearest, Hey Babe),
    I've waited (47,586 minutes, eons of time, since breakfast, 3.4 nanoseconds) to tell you how much you mean to (moi, our fifth period teacher, my little brother, your boyfriend). The reflection of (Saturn, your balding head, the grease on your nose, the swamp) shines in your eyes like the beautiful (banshees, SPAM, tadpoles, sludge) in the (sewer, ocean, dried lake, polluted river). Whenever I think of you, I think of (high-octane aftershave, deodorant,

(The sweetness continues on page 78!!)

hearts condemn us. For God is greater than our hearts, and he knows everything.

1 JOHN 3:19–20

It seems like I'm always wrestling with unreal fantasies. How can I control my thought life?

We demolish arguments and every pretension that sets itself up against the knowledge of God, and we take captive every thought to make it obedient to Christ.

2 CORINTHIANS 10:5

When girls wear revealing clothes, I have a difficult time with what goes through my mind. What should I do?

I made a covenant with my eyes not to look lustfully at a girl.

JOB 31:1

How can I avoid being influenced by this world and its perspective on sexuality?

For everything in the world—the cravings of sinful man, the lust of his eyes and the boasting of what he has and does—comes not from the Father but from the world.

1 JOHN 2:16

Living without Lust

The media has a big influence on me concerning sex. How can Jesus help me?

"I will remain in the world no longer, but they are still in the world, and I am coming to you. Holy Father, protect them by the power of your name—the name you gave me—so that they may be one as we are one."

JOHN 17:11

What does God say about sexual immorality?

Flee from sexual immorality. All other sins a man commits are outside his body, but he who sins sexually sins against his own body.

1 CORINTHIANS 6:18

I'm struggling with lust; what can I do?

How can a young man keep his way pure? By living according to your word.

PSALM 119:9

What does God want me to do with my body?

Do not offer the parts of your body to sin, as instruments of wickedness, but rather offer yourselves to God, as those who have been brought from death to life; and offer the parts of your body to him as instruments of righteousness.

ROMANS 6:13

Peer Pressure

Sex and Your Friends

Not me! Dating. Sex. Relationships. Sex. Friendships. Sex is just one of the things that friends normally talk, gossip, and create wild rumors about. The friends you choose will have a major influence on your sexual decisions. If your friends are sexually active, then

passion, nothing, Mrs. Paul's fish sticks), and I can't stop myself from (throwing up, laughing, screaming in pain, running). You actually don't even know me, but I know all about you and your (dark past, tattoo, Star Wars magazine subscription). I've watched you (pick your nose, laugh like a dying boar, phone 911, tease your dog), and I can't believe how much I want to speak with you (after eating cat food, alone in a deserted subway at 3:00 A.M., when I say so, in Irian Jaya). Meet me tonight (with a security guard, on Pan Am Flight 204, or else, I'm begging you). We could spend eternity (counting the hair follicles on our arms, playing squash or eating it, in straightjackets). There will never ever, ever be anyone who (washes their armpits, kneads bread, spills their guts, looks like a slobbering fool) like me. Until we rendezvous, I want you to (call the FBI, get braces, call me pooky, rent an ape suit).

Most (Passionately, Unworthily, Slovenly, Pathetically) Yours,

(That's all!)

you're going to face some tough choices. If your friends aren't sexually active, there will probably be less pressure on you to be sexually active. It works the other way too; your friends can get a lot of unnecessary pressure taken off them by the positive sexual decisions you choose to make. The struggle to be sexually active is an intense pressure that steams up a lot of young people. With God's help and his Word to give you the direction you need, you can be a positive influence on your friends concerning their sexual choices.

My best friend treats his girlfriend badly. What can I do?

Brothers, if someone is caught in a sin, you who are spiritual should restore him gently. But watch yourself, or you also may be tempted.

GALATIANS 6:1

What should I say to my friends when they brag about the girls they've had sex with?

Blessed is the man who does not walk in the counsel of the wicked or stand in the way of sinners or sit in the seat of mockers. But his delight is in the law of the LORD, and on his law he meditates day and night.

PSALM 1:1–2

A good friend of mine wants me to be more than a friend; how can I tell him that the feeling isn't mutual?

How painful are honest words!

JOB 6:25

I have a friend who is always dating, but I think she dates so much because she's insecure. How can I help her?

We who are strong ought to bear with the failings of the weak and not to please ourselves.

ROMANS 15:1

What can I say to my friends when they try to set me up with a girl I don't want to go out with?

Then do this, my son, to free yourself, since you have fallen into your neighbor's hands: Go and humble yourself; press your plea with your neighbor!

PROVERBS 6:3

What should I do when my friends call me a prude for not being sexually active?

"Blessed are you when people insult you, persecute you and falsely say all kinds of evil against you because of me."

MATTHEW 5:11

I'm concerned about a friend who's involved in a dangerous dating relationship; what should I say to him?

Yet do not regard him as an enemy, but warn him as a brother.

2 THESSALONIANS 3:15

My friend was sexually active and other kids in our youth group gossiped about her. What should I say to them?

"If any one of you is without sin, let him be the first to throw a stone at her."

JOHN 8:7

Outer Beauty

Mere Image

Mirror, mirror . . . There are lots of people on your campus who may appear gorgeous or handsome but are not necessarily attractive. Like a beautiful girl smoking a cigarette. Appears pretty? Yes. Attractive? Wheeze, hack, hack, wheeze. Or how about a football player with brontosaurus biceps but who smells like one too? Appears strong? Yes. Attractive? Get the Lysol! It's easy to think of appearance and attraction as similar items when you're checking out the dating menu. But before you order, be sure to know that appearance and attraction can be as different as anteaters and auks (a diving bird found in the northern seas, with webbed feet and short wings used as paddles). Attraction involves both inner and outer qualities and characteristics that cause other people to be drawn to you. However, appearance has to do with what you look like on the outside. God is more interested in your life being attractive than your face looking pretty. And he doesn't want you to be fooled by the mere image of appearance.

Should I be concerned that our society places so much emphasis on how you look and not on who you are?

But the Lord said to Samuel, . . . "The Lord does not look at the things man looks at. Man looks at the outward appearance, but the Lord looks at the heart."

1 Samuel 16:7

Guys are always telling me I have a great personality, but no one ever asks me out. How can I be patient?

Wait for the Lord; be strong and take heart and wait for the Lord.

Psalm 27:14

I know I'm not as pretty as other girls. What can I do to be beautiful in God's eyes?

Therefore, as God's chosen people, holy and dearly loved, clothe yourselves with compassion, kindness, humility, gentleness and patience.

COLOSSIANS 3:12

People are always telling me how pretty I am; why am I always the last to believe it?

Your beauty should not come from outward adornment, such as braided hair and the wearing of gold jewelry and fine clothes. Instead, it should be that of your inner self, the unfading beauty of a gentle and quiet spirit, which is of great worth in God's sight.

1 PETER 3:3–4

I'm not fat like I used to be, but I still feel fat inside. Does God still love me?

"Yet my unfailing love for you will not be shaken nor my covenant of peace be removed," says the LORD, who has compassion on you.

ISAIAH 54:10

The only way I can get a guy's attention is by wearing skimpy clothes. I know it's wrong, but what can I do to change?

Those who live according to the sinful nature have their minds set on what that nature desires; but those who live in

Outer Beauty 81

accordance with the Spirit have their minds set on what the Spirit desires.

ROMANS 8:5

I'm tired of trying to compete with others; is it right to see who can look the best?

Let us not become conceited, provoking and envying each other.

GALATIANS 5:26

Will I ever stop hating what I see when I stand in front of the mirror?

He has made everything beautiful in its time.

ECCLESIASTES 3:11

Tough Questions

Questions I'm Afraid to Ask

Have you ever been surrounded by brilliant people in one of your classes and been afraid to ask a question because you thought it was completely stupid? When it comes to asking questions about sex and feeling stupid, you're not alone. Thousands of students have millions upon jillions of questions about their bodies (and other people's bodies); but who wants to look like an uneducated, prudish idiot by asking a question? Here are some tough questions on some difficult subjects that I know many young people wrestle with on a daily basis.

I want to emphasize that if you have been a victim of sexual abuse (incest, rape, date rape, stepparent relationships), or if you're struggling with pornography or your sexual identity, you need to get help from someone you can trust, such as a parent, youth pastor, teacher, counselor, or some other caring adult. You do not have to suffer alone with pain and confusion. The following verses are meant to encourage you and remind you of God's promise to walk with you during your struggles. However, they are not a substitute for the wise counsel and advice of someone he wants to use to help you. Let God's Word comfort and encourage you. Let God's people help you walk with him through his process of healing your pain.

I've been sexually abused, and I need God's strength to tell someone about it. Will God help me?

"Do not be afraid, for I am with you."
ISAIAH 43:5

I just found out I tested positive for HIV; will God comfort me?

"Come to me, all you who are weary and burdened, and I will give you rest. Take my yoke upon you and learn from me, for I am gentle and humble in heart, and you will find rest for your souls. For my yoke is easy and my burden is light."
MATTHEW 11:28–30

I had an abortion, and I hate myself for it. Does God hate me too?

But now, this is what the Lord says—he who created you, O Jacob, he who formed you, O Israel: "Fear not, for I have redeemed you; I have summoned you by name; you are mine. When you pass through the waters, I will be with you; and when you pass through the rivers, they will not sweep over you. When you walk through the fire, you will not be burned; the flames will not set you ablaze."

ISAIAH 43:1–2

I found out that my father molested my sister; how can I forgive him?

Bear with each other and forgive whatever grievances you may have against one another. Forgive as the Lord forgave you.

COLOSSIANS 3:13

I have strong sexual feelings for people of the same sex. What can I do to be faithful to God?

"As the Father has loved me, so have I loved you. Now remain in my love."

JOHN 15:9

I'm struggling with pornographic web sites, adult movie channels, and porn videos. What should I do?

Do not lust in your heart after her beauty or let her captivate you with her eyes.

PROVERBS 6:25

I'm afraid to go to counseling for my sexual problems. Is counseling a very good idea?

For lack of guidance a nation falls, but many advisers make victory sure.

PROVERBS 11:14

I feel like I'm fighting a losing battle; will I ever overcome being so promiscuous?

For everyone born of God overcomes the world. This is the victory that has overcome the world, even our faith.

1 JOHN 5:4

3

Family Frustrations

Moving brings out the worst in me. Packing boxes. Lifting. Grunting. Throwing out old stuff I don't need. Leaving old friends. Cleaning. Digging through piles of junk I'd rather just leave as piles of junk. Breaking things. Organizing the unorganizable. Unpacking. Unpacking the piles of junk I reluctantly decided to bring with me. Having leery new neighbors stare at me as if I had antennas on my head. *Hi, my name's George Jetson. What's yours?*

Moving is a frustrating process. There never seems to be a right time, enough people to help, or an easy way to do it. Moving is hard work. It's difficult on everyone. Teenagers. Parents. Little brothers and sisters. (Scratch that last one . . . all they do is sit around playing while you do all the work.) Transporting truckloads of stuff from one location to another unpacks emotions most of us would rather leave at home. Sadness over losing friends. Anger over wondering why your dad's company moves families around like pawns on a chessboard. Resentment because you have to do more work than your brother. Grief over having to give away a favorite pet. Feeling like the decision is out of your control. Moving can scatter family members in many different directions. The challenge to making a major move is being sure that the whole family is moving in the same direction.

Moving is all about change, and change is what families are all about. Families are in a constant, lifelong process of moving and changing. That can be a sign of a healthy family. Change brings about growth and moving shows progress. If it's in the right direction. Many of today's families are changing and moving in the wrong direction. Divorce. Physical abuse. Emotional abuse. Sexual abuse. Silence. Workaholism. Affairs. Unrealistic expectations.

Some of these moves are unavoidable, and many of them are not your fault. Divorce is a move your parents decide on and not you. Abuse is a move someone inflicts on you or another family member. Living with a dad who never tells you that he loves you is his bad move, not yours. A family doesn't need to move across the country to make a bad move. Plenty of bad moves are made by families who never move at all. When a family isn't moving in a positive direction, it produces changes that create the worst in people. That's a bad move.

You can help your family head in the right direction by following God's direction for your life. It may change your family. If it doesn't, at least it will move you in the right direction. God cares about your family. He cares about you. He wants to see you making moves that bring you closer to him and your family. If you have a family that you feel will never change, at least you can allow God to make changes in your life. If you've come from a good family that still has its frustrations, his Word can help you deal with problems in a constructive way. God wants to use you to help construct a healthy family. You are a key part of his family building plan.

In your family, you have the choice to be part of the construction team or the destruction team. It takes a lot longer to build a house than to demolish it. A wrecking ball weighs tons more than a hammer, but a wrecking ball serves only one purpose. Do you want to be a hammer or a wrecking ball? Do you want to help move your family to make positive changes or negative ones? This chapter will give you the tools you need from God's Word to be an expert builder. You've also got the help of a master builder who knows a lot about carpentry. Jesus will help you be a positive influence in your family for change. His Word will help you lay a foundation for your life. When the family frustrations you encounter beat against your house, you'll be able to stand firm on a strong foundation. That's a change that'll create the best in you and hopefully your family too. That's a move in the right direction.

Stepfamilies

Blended Family Blues

Divorce stinks. I can't think of anything that ruins families more than divorce. Helping students deal with their parents' divorce and the awkwardness of seeing their parents remarry has been one of my biggest challenges as a youth minister. One thing I've discovered about students from divorced homes is that everyone's situation is different. Parents with teenagers who divorce and remarry can provide wonderful homes for their kids. The opposite is also true. Blended families can produce a lot of mixed feelings and awkwardness for young people. Stepmoms, stepdads, stepbrothers and sisters, stepgrandmas . . . without any decision on your part, you inherit a whole family of steps. What about your new stepbrother who's a creep? What about spending the weekend at your dad's house? Before, you kept your clothes in one house, but now you're living out of a suitcase as you bounce back and forth between homes.

If you're in a blended family, you know what the endless issues are: holidays, communication, discipline, new ways of doing things, wondering where you fit in, etc. Whether you have a good or bad stepfamily situation, God understands how you feel. In fact, the Bible says that God hates divorce because it's not part of his plan. He can't stand seeing people hurt one another, and he understands what separation feels like. As you read through these situations, some of them may apply to you while others won't. But catch this one truth: Out of the millions of divorced families, God specifically cares about you and your family.

My father died when I was young, and now I have a step-dad who couldn't care less about me. Can God be the dad I don't have?

For you did not receive a spirit that makes you a slave again to fear, but you received the Spirit of sonship. And by him we cry, "*Abba,* Father." The Spirit himself testifies with our spirit that we are God's children.

ROMANS 8:15–16

I have nobody to talk to at my house. My parents are remarried, but they both spend all their time thinking about their new mates; will Jesus hear what I have to say when no one else will?

This is the confidence we have in approaching God: that if we ask anything according to his will, he hears us.

1 JOHN 5:14

My stepfamily is so messed up nobody knows how to talk to each other. How can I get everyone together?

Getting Nailed

If Tiffany Daniels only knew. All semester long you've stared at her pretty brown eyes, long golden hair, and shimmering white teeth, but you've been too chicken to ask her out. *She'd never go out with me,* you mourn to yourself. You know you lack the needed charm, studly body, clever wit, and all the other required credentials, including money, to get her to go out with you. You have nothing to offer her. EXCEPT . . . you have something Tiffany needs: your brains.

You spent all last night studying for your history test. Shunning your favorite TV program, you meticulously memorized every significant event, important name, and bloody battle of the Revolutionary War. Confidence overflows in every step you take as you march into third period. Your brains are loaded, armed, and ready to fire away at every multiple-choice, fill-in-the-blank, matching column, vocabulary definition, and essay your

(Keep going!!)

teacher launches at you. You are ready for war.

Sitting down, you glance over at Tiffany and say, "Hi! Ready for the test?" With a pouty, teary-eyed expression, she slowly turns toward you and says, "No, I'm probably going to fail. I studied for so many hours, but all these people and dates and battles just confuse me. If I don't pass this test, I'll have to go to summer school. I don't know what I'm going to do." She folds her arms on her desk and buries her head in frustration. *Aha! Time to make my move!*

Minutes later, tests have been passed out and pencils are scratching away. Your teacher announces he has to step out for a couple minutes and holds the class to its honor. You are ready to honor Tiffany with your expansive wisdom. Your answers are going to win you major extra credit with her.

You thought your teacher was out of sight. You thought you'd never

(More on page 92!!)
☞

Let us then approach the throne of grace with confidence, so that we may receive mercy and find grace to help us in our time of need.

HEBREWS 4:16

My stepdad never has a positive thing to say to me; all he ever does is cut me down. Where can I turn?

For the LORD comforts his people and will have compassion on his afflicted ones.

ISAIAH 49:13

How can I handle all the hassles in my step-family?

Be on your guard; stand firm in the faith; be men of courage; be strong.

1 CORINTHIANS 16:13

I can't stand my stepbrothers. Will it ever be possible for me to get along with them?

When a man's ways are pleasing to the LORD, he makes even his enemies live at peace with him.

PROVERBS 16:7

What should I do to develop a better relationship with my stepmom?

Live in peace with each other.

1 THESSALONIANS 5:13

I feel rejected by my real parents and my step-parents. Has anyone in the Bible ever felt rejected like this?

Stepfamilies

Do not hide your face from me, do not turn your servant away in anger; you have been my helper. Do not reject me or forsake me, O God my Savior.

.PSALM 27:9

My mom always sides with my stepfather and never sticks up for me. Will God stick up for me when no one else will?

The LORD is with me; he is my helper.

PSALM 118:7

Getting Busted

Cruel and Unusual Punishment

House arrest. Restriction. Grounded for life. A stiff sentence. Electronic surveillance. You've been nailed for a no-no, and now you've got to pay.

When you get grounded, parents get the incredible distinction of playing prosecutor, judge, and jury. They state the alleged crime, present the evidence, listen to the defendant's case, deliberate on a decision, and cast the sentence. The only thing you get to be is the criminal and defense attorney with a losing argument. The defendant is guilty as charged. BAM! Case closed.

Parents are often accused of cruel and unusual punishment in sentencing their very own offspring. No car for a month. No going out on the weekend. No phone. Come right home after school. More chores. Remember that ski trip with your friends? Sorry, it's just been canceled. You wonder, "Would a ball and chain be easier?" And what about when your brother or sister gets in trouble? They never get it half as bad as you do!

Getting sentenced to stare at your bedroom ceiling is a drag, but part of breaking the law of the land means being able to accept the consequences. Why do parents ground perfectly good teenagers? I don't have all the answers, but God's Word

get caught! WRONG! You
failed to realize that teachers have a sixth
sense for smelling conspicuous conspiracies like cheating. You forgot that the classroom door has a little rectangular
window. You weren't looking out. Your teacher was looking in. You
didn't hear the classroom door open. You felt a sinister presence behind
you. Only after you heard your teacher say sharply, "Mr. Maciborski, I'd like
to speak with you and Miss Daniels immediately after class," did a little tiny
voice type this red alert message in your brain 4.8 seconds too late: "Y-O-U-'R-E-
N-A-I-L-E-D!"
When was the last time you got nailed? What'd you do? Break curfew?
Mouth off to your teacher? Just short of twisting thumb cuffs and electric
shock therapy, teachers and parents promise all sorts of heinous behav-
ior modification techniques to remind you what you did. And to
make sure it never happens again.

(There's more!!)

has some specific reasons for discipline, consequences, and learning to make good decisions. If you're confined to house arrest, here's where the Bible can shine some light on your dark, dingy, rat-infested prison cell. (P.S. Don't try to escape . . . prisoners have been shot for less than that!)

My friends don't obey their parents, and they don't get in trouble; why should I obey mine?

Children, obey your parents in the Lord, for this is right.

EPHESIANS 6:1

My parents are so strict; why won't they let me do anything?

Listen, my son, to your father's instruction and do not for-sake your mother's teaching. They will be a garland to grace your head and a chain to adorn your neck.

PROVERBS 1:8–9

Why do parents discipline their kids?

Getting Busted

He who spares the rod hates his son, but he who loves him is careful to discipline him.

PROVERBS 13:24

My dad says I'm supposed to be a good example to my younger brothers and sisters. Why?

He who heeds discipline shows the way to life, but whoever ignores correction leads others astray.

PROVERBS 10:17

My friend always gets in trouble with his folks. Why doesn't he learn from his mistakes?

He who ignores discipline despises himself, but whoever heeds correction gains understanding.

PROVERBS 15:32

Why do I have to get grounded for messing up?

If you are not disciplined (and everyone undergoes discipline), then you are illegitimate children and not true sons.

HEBREWS 12:8

Why does God discipline us?

Our fathers disciplined us for a little while as they thought best; but God disciplines us for our good, that we may share in his holiness.

HEBREWS 12:10

If you've been busted, turned in, or seen your face on *America's Most Wanted,* here are some critical suggestions about making your next few moves. First of all, whatever you do, don't plead the fifth, ask to see a lawyer, go looking for your passport, and hold a press conference. You don't even want to ask for your rights to be read; you don't have any rights. Remember, you've been nailed. Prisoners have no rights.

Instead of copping a bunch of lame excuses that make no sense to anyone but you, the first, best, and hardest thing to do is admit that you've been nailed. In other words, plead guilty. That way you can head right to the trial and sentencing. Attempting to blame others, avoiding responsibility, or adjusting the story to make you or the incident not look so bad only drags the problem out. And that's a drag for your mom, dad, teacher, coach, vice-principal, or police officer, the very people you don't want to upset any more than they are. Admitting you're wrong is the first step to resolving the chaos you just created.

The next step you want to take is accepting the consequences for your actions. You see, you may be willing to admit you've been nailed, but accepting the consequences for what you've done is a much bigger step than a lot of guys are willing to take. Consequences are a part of the real

(Check out page 95!!)

☞

Positive Influence

Family Fitness

One, two, three . . . Are you making your family stronger or weaker? Are you a team player? Are you a positive, contributing member of your family? Everything you say and do in your family makes a difference. Yes . . . EVERYTHING! It's easy to forget what a powerful influence you can exert on your family. It's also really easy to forget that attitudes, words, actions, slipups, mistakes, and deliberate acts of unkindness affect how others treat you. God wants you to be a change-maker in your family. You're the person he has chosen to bring peace to a tension-filled home. He wants you to encourage your dad instead of mouthing off to him. He wants you to break up that fight between your brother and sister. (Step in when the coast is clear!) God's Word has plenty of character-building carbos for you to feast on so you can make your family stronger. Dig in and get yourself in shape!

What can I do to help out my sister who's going through a hard time?

But encourage one another daily.

HEBREWS 3:13

I'm trying to change my negative attitudes around home, but how can I avoid getting stuck in the same old patterns?

You were taught, with regard to your former way of life, to put off your old self, which is being corrupted by its deceitful desires; to be made new in the attitude of your minds; and to put on the new self, created to be like God in true righteousness and holiness.

EPHESIANS 4:22–24

Positive Influence

world, and accepting consequences means paying for what you've broken, apologizing for what you've said or done, and accepting any punishment for your crimes against humanity. Okay, maybe just crimes against your sister.

Lawyers, parole officers, and bail bondsmen can give you all sorts of legal counsel after you've been nailed, but the best advice comes from 1 John 1:9. John says, "If we confess our sins, he is faithful and just and will forgive us our sins and purify us from all unrighteousness." Why is that the best advice? After admitting your crime of paint-balling your neighbor's cat or stealing an NFL hat, you may still be carrying guilt that's gouging holes in your heart. After accepting the consequence of being sentenced to your room until next winter, there still may be the possibility that you've got unfinished business with God. That's where confession comes in. Confession isn't just admitting, and it's not just accepting. It's agreeing with God that you're wrong. You can admit and not agree . . . and you can accept and still not agree. Confessing means a wholehearted, 100 percent, unconditional agreement that God is right and you are wrong. Confession is admitting, accepting, and agreeing. The whole enchilada.

Jesus is not like a lawyer who bills at $200 an hour. He's not like a Santa Claus parole officer to see if you've been naughty or nice. He's not a bail bondsman who wants to make sure you won't skip town. Jesus Christ, the Son of the living God, was beat up, bruised, and bloodied for your sins and mine. Even though he was innocent, Jesus admitted, accepted, and agreed with God that something had to be done for all the stinking sin in this world. Jesus didn't have to confess to any sins, yet he still died on a cross for you. His crucifixion cost him his life and you nothing. Jesus was crucified so that you could experience the freedom of his Father's forgiveness. No matter what you've done, you can freely confess your sins to him. He is faithful and just to forgive you. He didn't get nailed for nothing. Jesus got nailed for you.

(That's all!)

How to Get Permission to Do Just About Anything

When was the last time you were denied permission to go . . .

- Out with your friends?
- To the movies?
- To the bathroom?
- To a Wrestlemania Slugfest?
- To Paris for the weekend?
- Anywhere?

If you want to learn how to get permission to do just about anything, like bungee jumping over flaming vats of vegetable oil, then read on.

(Don't stop here!!)

☞

How can I be a positive influence in my family?

Therefore encourage one another and build each other up, just as in fact you are doing.

1 THESSALONIANS 5:11

My little sister always wants to spend time with me. What should I do?

Each of you should look not only to your own interests, but also to the interests of others.

PHILIPPIANS 2:4

Positive Influence

I want to change the way I act at home; where's a good place to start?

Do everything without complaining or arguing.

PHILIPPIANS 2:14

My mom is depressed about her recent divorce. How can I help her?

A cheerful heart is good medicine, but a crushed spirit dries up the bones.

PROVERBS 17:22

How can I show my parents I appreciate all the things they do for me?

Be thankful.

COLOSSIANS 3:15

What are some positive qualities that'll help me make a difference in my family?

To be obedient, to be ready to do whatever is good, to slander no one, to be peaceable and considerate, and to show true humility toward all men.

TITUS 3:1–2

Most teenagers (I know that assumption strikes to the very core of your individuality) have parents they report to. *Check in; check out. Write a note. Call my pager number. Call me on the cell phone. Phone home if you're going to be late or else!* Getting permission to do something is a parent's way of knowing what's going on in your life when you leave home. Some young people can't understand why their parents are concerned about alcohol. Or those one-ton hunks of high-velocity steel called "cars." Or hormones. Or your friends whom they don't know. A parent who asks good questions is a parent who's doing their job right. So you want to go out Friday night? Here are some practical ways to get permission to do practically anything that is safe, legal, and fun.

ESTABLISH TRUST: EARN THE RIGHT TO GET PERMISSION

There's more to getting the car than bringing it back clean and with gas in the

(More on page 99!!)
☞

Words That Kill

Going Ballistic

What's the deal?

Smart weapons rarely miss their targets. Fiber-optic visibility. A tonnage of big-bang stuff. A brain kinda like Einstein's. These smart weapons will fly up a Volkswagen tailpipe in Missouri if steered in the right direction. The Persian Gulf War featured the intricate technology and precision of radar-guided missiles. Our words, especially cruel words, are just like smart weapons. Words meant to hurt have destructive power that cripples human targets. What comes out of the mouth can launch exploding aerial attacks right to the heart. Like the latest high-tech video game, the tongue is the cruelest joystick around.

Going ballistic with your mouth is a dangerous war game. Words can backfire and explode in your face. If they hit their target, casualties can be severe. If you make a habit of going ballistic, you'd better take cover quick, because your friends will either launch their own offensive or retreat to find new friends. Once you press the launch button, the missile's heat-sensing lock is irreversible. You can't retrieve it. Smoke and rubble litter the impact zone. The damage has been done.

Fortunately, because of Jesus Christ's death and resurrection, God provides the cleanup crew of grace and forgiveness. Admitting your out-of-control tongue inflicted unnecessary damage is the first step toward healing the wound. God is ready and willing to forgive ballistic blunders. He wants you to be wise with your words so you can target your tongue toward peace.

How can I keep from always getting in trouble for talking back to my parents?

When words are many, sin is not absent, but he who holds his tongue is wise.

PROVERBS 10:19

My dad is always telling me to do what he says. Why do I have to?

Stop listening to instruction, my son, and you will stray from the words of knowledge.

PROVERBS 19:27

My parents are always telling me to think before I speak. How can I say things in the right way?

A word aptly spoken is like apples of gold in settings of silver.

PROVERBS 25:11

I hurt my sister by saying something unkind. How can I change the way I speak to her?

Pleasant words are a honeycomb, sweet to the soul and healing to the bones.

PROVERBS 16:24

My brother is always blaming me for things he did. Did anyone in the Bible ever go through that?

All day long they twist my words; they are always plotting to harm me.

PSALM 56:5

tank. Trust is probably the strongest criterion a parent uses when giving permission. If you're trustworthy, that means you're worth trusting. Trust is earned by keeping promises, following through on what you said you'd do, and by making sure if you break your parents' trust, you own up to it quickly. Being a teenager doesn't guarantee you anything (sorry!), but being trustworthy can earn your parents' respect. If your parents don't trust you, ask yourself one simple question, "What have I done to earn their trust?"

DEVELOP YOUR GAME PLAN: KNOW THE FIVE W'S (WHO, WHAT, WHEN, WHY, WHERE)

Friday Night Scenario #3758496785—Teenager Pleading for House Leave

"Mom, can I go out with Tom tonight?"

"What are you going to do?"

"I don't know. We're supposed to go over to Bob's house."

(Good stuff, huh! Read on!!)

☞

"Bob who?"

"I don't know; he's a friend of Susan's."

"Susan who?"

"Some girl in Bob's science class."

"Where does Bob live?"

"Somewhere near town."

"You'll have to be a little more specific than that; which town?"

"The town Bob lives in!"

"When are you going to be home?"

"Before sunrise."

"Forget it."

Answer the Five W's. *Whatever you do, answer the Five W's.* In most cases, they are your ticket out the door. Forget the Five W's, and you'll have to resort to Friday Night Scenario #3758496786: "Mom, can Bob come over tonight?"

HANG OUT WITH FRIENDS YOUR PARENTS TRUST

Back to the trust issue. If your parents know and like your friends (Remember: knowing and liking can be diametrically opposed), you're off to a very good start. If your friends want to impress your parents, tell them to slow down to sixty-five mph before they pull up in front of your house. Ask your friends to be willing to talk with your folks. Your friends can make you look very trustworthy or very irresponsible. Parents often gauge maturity on the basis of how well you pick your friends. You need friends you can trust. If you want to go somewhere for the weekend or out to a party, your parents need to know your friends are trustworthy. Trustworthy like you.

DO YOUR WORK (SCHOOLWORK, CHORES, WATERING THE CAT . . . GET IT DONE!)

"Mom, can I go outside to play?" "Not until you clean your room." You've heard it since you were little. You want to do something or go somewhere? Clean your room. Clean the kitchen. Clean the yard. Wash the dog. Scrub the toilets. Do your wash. Finish your homework. Doing your work, whatever the work is, shows your parents that you're a team player. Responsibility has its benefits. And irresponsibility has its consequences. Getting permission to do just about anything begins with doing the right things first. The choice begins with you.

(That's all!)

Words That Kill

How can I learn to communicate calmly instead of always yelling and screaming?

The quiet words of the wise are more to be heeded than the shouts of a ruler of fools.

ECCLESIASTES 9:17

How can I stop lying to my parents?

Whoever of you loves life and desires to see many good days, keep your tongue from evil and your lips from speaking lies.

PSALM 34:12–13

Does God really know what I'm going to say before I say it?

Before a word is on my tongue you know it completely, O LORD.

PSALM 139:4

Family Struggles

Growing Pains

Never has there been such a crippling force or destructive energy as the power of pain. It doesn't take long in working with young people to discover that pain is a regular part of their lives. Not every student comes from a lousy family, but there are many who do. Alcoholic parents. Abusive parents. Parents who mortgage their kids for their job. Divorce. Affairs. The list goes on and on. Parents in pain. Kids in pain. Whole families in pain. How can destructive family pain be turned into a healthy type of growing pain?

You may not know what growing pains are, but when I was a kid, I got 'em all the time. At night my leg muscles would throb with a grinding sort of pain that made me feel like I was on a medieval torture rack. I remember crying in my bed, rolling back and forth, wishing the pain would go away. My mom would come into the room and try to work out the soreness by massaging my legs, or she'd make me sit in a tub of warm water. I couldn't figure out what made my legs feel like they'd been run over by a tank. All I knew was the pain. My legs were killing me.

Growing pains are a lot easier to deal with than family pains. Growing pains go away. Family pains tend to stick around longer. Sitting in a tub of warm water won't ease your family pains, but by his Spirit, God can bring miraculous comfort and healing to your family. This stretching, pulling, ripping time you're going through won't last forever. Even if you can't understand why God has allowed certain things to happen in your family, understand that he is with you in your pain. He wants to encourage you and give you hope through his Word. Your growing pains can make you stronger and develop you into the person God wants you to become. Let his gentle hands massage the hurts in your heart.

Does God understand how bad my family situation really is?

I will be glad and rejoice in your love, for you saw my affliction and knew the anguish of my soul.

PSALM 31:7

Can I count on God to help me with my family problems?

Then they cried to the LORD in their trouble, and he saved them from their distress.

PSALM 107:19

Will the pain in my family ever end?

Family Struggles

He will wipe every tear from their eyes. There will be no more death or mourning or crying or pain, for the old order of things has passed away.

REVELATION 21:4

My family problems affect everything I do and am. Can God keep me from giving up?

For you, O LORD, have delivered my soul from death, my eyes from tears, my feet from stumbling.

PSALM 116:8

Does God love me and care for me even though my parents don't?

He tends his flock like a shepherd: He gathers the lambs in his arms and carries them close to his heart; he gently leads those that have young.

ISAIAH 40:11

My friends come from good homes and can't relate to how bad my family problems are. Can God relate to my pain?

I will be glad and rejoice in your love, for you saw my affliction and knew the anguish of my soul.

PSALM 31:7

Should I trust God with my family problems?

In that day they will say, "Surely this is our God; we trusted in him,

Father's Day without Dad

Father's Day 1992. That's the day PJ Kerr's dad discovered he had an incurable brain tumor.

Father's Day 1993. PJ spent Father's Day without his dad. PJ's dad died ten months earlier on August 21st. The day after his mom's birthday.

Facing his first Father's Day without his dad, PJ said, "All my friends were talking about what they were going to do for Father's Day, and I just sat there thinking, *What am I going to do?*"

What am I going to do? That's a hard question. For most guys, spending Father's Day without Dad is a drag. It can mean feeling alone and left out when everyone else is having a good time. Even though it may not be cool to

(Turn to page 105)

Family Struggles

and he saved us. This is the Lord, we trusted in him; let us rejoice and be glad in his salvation."

Isaiah 25:9

Family Living

Jell-O through a Straw

If only... When was the last time you shook a bowlful of lime Jell-O that was covered with mini-marshmallows? Shake any part of the bowl, and every single marshmallow in the green goo will wobble. That's what a family is like. Whenever one part moves, the whole thing moves. Some people call it a family system. I call it Jell-O. Every person in the family is interrelated, interconnected, interimportant, and interdependent. It doesn't matter if you're Mom, Dad, sister, brother, adopted, step, or pet. Each person affects everyone else. No action or decision is made without having some type of impact on the whole bowl, er, family. Wobble-wobble.

Whether you realize it or not, your decisions affect your whole family. That's why God places so much importance on things like obedience, listening to Mom or Dad, attitudes, and being a contributor instead of a leech. If you blow off your folks, ignore what they ask you to do, or mouth off, life in your family will definitely not gel. God doesn't tell you to obey your parents for blind obedience's sake. He says it because obedience pleases him. If you really want to please God, then be willing to obey your parents.

God has a ton of blessings ready for you when you obey. On the other hand, the consequences for being a rotten marshmallow are endless. Trying to do your own thing in your family while trying to live for God just won't work. It'll be as difficult as sucking Jell-O through a straw.

Must I always listen to what my parents have to say?

Listen to your father, who gave you life, and do not despise your mother when she is old.

PROVERBS 23:22

What does the Bible say about father/son relationships?

The father of a righteous man has great joy; he who has a wise son delights in him.

PROVERBS 23:24

Why do my parents always say, "We told you so . . ."?

The way of a fool seems right to him, but a wise man listens to advice.

PROVERBS 12:15

What can I do when no one in my family listens to me?

O LORD, hear my prayer, listen to my cry for mercy; in your faithfulness and righteousness come to my relief.

PSALM 143:1

Why do kids have to obey their parents?

Listen to advice and accept instruction, and in the end you will be wise.

PROVERBS 19:20

My parents tell me I'm a great talker but a lousy listener. What does God have to say about me being a better listener?

He who answers before listening—that is his folly and his shame.

PROVERBS 18:13

admit it, Father's Day can be a bummer time of difficult memories, feelings of loss, anger, frustration, and wondering why everybody's dad is around but yours. And speaking of dads, where does God, your heavenly Father, fit in all this? What difference does God make when your earthly dad isn't around to hang out with anymore?

To tackle this tough topic, we decided to talk to a couple guys who face Father's Day every year without their dads. STATS: (1) PJ Kerr . . . seventeen . . . basketball player . . . Dad got cancer. (2) Jared Anderson . . . fifteen . . . weight lifter/artist . . . Dad was a dropout surfer. PJ and Jared's experiences can help you look at Father's Day in a new way, so Father's Day doesn't have to be a drag.

Traditionally, Father's Day has been that once-a-year day to be cool to your dad by buying him a new putter, 2,381-piece tool set, or the latest style of bowling shoes. No matter

(Keep reading!!)
☞

Family Living

how good or bad a dad is the other 364 days, Father's Day will always be the one day that we are obligated as their biological offspring to say "Thanks for being my dad." What is a guy supposed to do when Dad, the focus of the celebration, is either dead, divorced, or dropped out?

After PJ's dad died, it took him about six months to talk about his dad's death.

PJ: *I didn't want to deal with it. I stuffed a lot of feelings. I didn't want to talk to anyone. There were more important things than talking about my dad's death.*

One night, I was sitting at home watching TV when, all of a sudden, an image of him popped into my head, an image of his dead body in bed, and all of a sudden I started crying.

My mom asked, "What's wrong?" I answered, "I miss him."

PJ's dad was someone he could always talk to. Even though his parents were divorced, PJ spoke with his dad on the phone a couple times a week.

My dad was the person I could go to for anything. I always had the feeling that my dad was right behind my shoul-der, always there for me for anything. My dad would always come down for Father's Day. Those were good days.

What does PJ recommend for guys like him, whose dads have passed away and aren't around on Father's Day?

Don't let your emotions bottle up inside. When I did that, I just became miserable. Talk to people. Let out whatever feelings you have. The longer you hold them in, the harder it will be to let them out.

Jared's parents divorced when he was one. His dad was a nineteen-year-old surfer who felt that work was for people who didn't know how to surf. Since he has never met his biological father, Jared has always had a different sort of Father's Day. Fortunately, Jared has developed a great relationship with his stepdad, Terry.

Jared: *Terry is pretty much the only dad I've ever known. We go to see movies, we like to play catch outside on the week-*

(More to follow!!)

I hate it when my parents are always right. I know they're just looking out for me, but do I have to listen to them?

Like an earring of gold or an ornament of fine gold is a wise man's rebuke to a listening ear.

PROVERBS 25:12

My brother and I get in fights all the time. How can we control our tempers?

A hot-tempered man stirs up dissension, but a patient man calms a quarrel.

PROVERBS 15:18

Family Living

Telling Lies

Lying through Your Teeth

Truth is good. What if the smell of your breath gave away your lies? If lies produced smells, they'd be a mix of sewage, rotten onions, minced garlic, B.O., Limburger cheese, cigarette butts, and a splash of barf. Why? Because lies stink. Half-truths, little white lies, cover-ups, and distorted images of what the real truth is are subtle and not-so-subtle ways to save our skin. "But if I told the truth about what really happened, my parents would kill me!" you say. Maybe so, but probably not.

Parents want to know the truth. You know how it goes: The whole truth and nothing but the truth. Students who struggle with lying to their parents never seem to figure out that truth builds exactly what they're looking for: trust. Trust is based

ends, and we go to Disneyland. We even had a really good time going to a concert together.

The very week before this article was written, Jared saw, for the first time, a picture of his real dad.

This past Friday, my mom gave me a picture of my biological father. She found it in one of my great-grandma's albums. That was the first time I had ever seen a photo of my real father. When my mom went into the bank and I stayed in the car, I started crying because that was the first time I ever saw a picture of him.

Father's Day is different at Jared's home because Jared never sees his biological father. Still, Jared is able to celebrate Father's Day with his stepdad and grandfather by doing the "present-and-dinner-thing."

Even if your real dad has died, gotten divorced, or dropped out like Jared's and PJ's dads, there's still hope. Father's Day doesn't have to be a drag when you know you have a heavenly Father who cares about you. God is someone who listens to you when you're bummed, understands when you're angry (even if you're angry at God), and knows when words can't describe how much you miss your dad.

On Father's Day, PJ and Jared know that God is the One who fills a big gap that was once reserved for their dads.

(One more to go!!)

☞

upon telling the truth. I don't know how many times I've heard students say, "But my parents don't trust me, and they never will." If your mom and dad have a hard time trusting you, is it because there's a rotten smell floating out of your mouth? Have you given them any reason to trust you? Do you have a history of telling lies? Are you digging your own grave with your tongue?

God's Word talks a lot about honesty, integrity, lying, and the rotten breath it produces. Telling the truth to your parents may not win brownie points with your friends, but it may develop the type of trust that is critical to healthy relationships. Truth telling produces trust. Telling lies breeds rotten relationships, yet most parents won't resort to washing a sixteen-year-old's mouth out with soap. Next time a lie is ready to slither off your tongue, just remember that blowing soap bubbles isn't much better than sewer breath.

Jared: *God makes a major difference in my life. So you won't be so bummed out on Father's Day, look to the future and let God take care of your problems for you.*

PJ: *Whenever my dad came over, we'd spend the time talking and playing basketball. When I miss him, I remember the good times we had and I play basketball. I pretend I'm playing basketball with him one-on-one, even though no one's there. I just pretend we're playing one-on-one together. Now that my dad is gone, God has taken my father's place; he watches over me in everything.*

PJ wants to be a basketball coach someday. With words like that, he can coach my kid any day. Those words are the best Father's Day gift his dad and God could ever receive.

(That's all!)

How can God's Word help me to be honest?

Keep me from deceitful ways; be gracious to me through your law. I have chosen the way of truth; I have set my heart on your laws.

PSALM 119:29–30

I didn't realize that lying to my mom would hurt her so bad. I feel awful for not telling the truth; how can I learn from this?

The tongue that brings healing is a tree of life, but a deceitful tongue crushes the spirit.

PROVERBS 15:4

Telling Lies

*Why is it easy to lie and so hard to
tell the truth?*

> The heart is deceitful above
> all things and beyond cure.
> Who can understand it?
>> JEREMIAH 17:9

*My parents and even people
in our neighborhood don't
trust me because I've built a
reputation for being a liar.
What can I do to change?*

> Therefore each of you must
> put off falsehood and speak truth-
> fully to his neighbor, for we are all
> members of one body.
>> EPHESIANS 4:25

*All my friends lie to their parents and never get in trouble. Is telling
the truth worth it?*

> "Whoever would love life and see good days must keep his
> tongue from evil and his lips from deceitful speech."
>> 1 PETER 3:10

*My brother is doing things I know he's not supposed to; if my
parents ask me about it, what should I tell them?*

> These are the things you are to do: Speak the truth to each
> other.
>> ZECHARIAH 8:16

*I've been forging notes at school since I was a freshman, and I
haven't been caught yet. Nobody knows, so what's the big deal?*

> A false witness will not go unpunished, and he who pours
> out lies will perish.
>> PROVERBS 19:9

Telling Lies

*My parents caught me lying to them. I know lying hurts them,
but how can it really hurt me?*

Do not deceive yourselves. If any one of you thinks he is
wise by the standards of this age, he should become a "fool"
so that he may become wise.

1 CORINTHIANS 3:18

Sibling Rivalry

Man against Monster

I remember the day my brother Neil almost met his Maker. When we were kids, Saturday afternoons were spent watching cheesy, old karate movies. You know, the Academy Award–winning movies of Bruce Lee and Chuck Norris that are famous for the sound coming two seconds after the actor's lips move. One day, Neil and I were out in front of the house, and he somehow thought he was Bruce Lee. We were goof-
ing around, and he launched a fake
karate kick into my face. The only
problem was that his shoe didn't stay
on his foot. By accident, his shoe
rocketed off and hit me in the
mouth! Joey O'Connor became
Godzilla. Have you ever seen a
Bruce Lee versus Godzilla movie?
Man against monster is a rather ugly
sight. Years have passed since that last
altercation, and Neil's recovery has been
slow but steady. Although he now walks with a
slight limp, he's fortunate to be able to kick off his shoes.

Sibling rivalry has been around for a long time. Cain took things too far when he killed his brother, Abel. David's brothers

Sibling Rivalry

laughed at him when he wanted to take on Goliath. Joseph, the dream boy, got pounded and thrown into an empty well for wearing color-coordinated clothes. His taste for high fashion did not impress his brothers. Sibling rivalry is part of growing up, and if you have brothers and sisters, you know what I mean. Teasing, "borrowing" things that aren't yours, saying unkind words, being jealous, and engaging in fierce competitions are only a few ways that brothers and sisters establish territory and bragging rights. Lucky parents get to be referees, making calls that don't always go your way.

God wants you to be a peacemaker instead of a troublemaker. Even though there are always going to be fights, disagreements, shouting matches, and hurt feelings, God wants you to work out your problem so hurt doesn't turn into hatred. First John 4:20 says, "If anyone says, 'I love God,' yet hates his brother, he is a liar. For anyone who does not love his brother, whom he has seen, cannot love God, whom he has not seen." God's serious about our loving the brothers and sisters he's given us. Don't let flying shoes karate chop your relationship in two.

What can I do when my brother is constantly picking on me?

Do not repay anyone evil for evil.

ROMANS 12:17

Where is God when my sister spends hours in the bathroom? She says, "Girls need more time to get ready in the morning." She never thinks of others, only herself.

Be devoted to one another in brotherly love. Honor one another above yourselves.

ROMANS 12:10

How to Make Your Parents Stop the Car

When you were a small child, how many times did you hear your mother scream, "Don't make me stop this car . . . don't make me stop this car"? If you're having trouble getting your parents' attention, what worked as a kid will still work for you as a teenager. If you really wanna know how to stop the car, this stuff'll make 'em slam on the brakes.

- Read them your report card.
- Take off your baby sister's dirty diaper.
- Throw your dog's ball out the window. . . . "Go get it, Skippy!"

(One to go!!)

My older brother gets all the attention because he's a great athlete and I'm not; why won't anyone recognize me for who I am or what I do?

Yet the LORD longs to be gracious to you; he rises to show you compassion. For the LORD is a God of justice. Blessed are all who wait for him!

ISAIAH 30:18

Is it fair that, just because I'm older than my sister, I automatically get in trouble for things she does?

Let us therefore make every effort to do what leads to peace and to mutual edification.

ROMANS 14:19

My older brother is in trouble with the law; how can I help him?

If any of you lacks wisdom, he should ask God, who gives generously to all without finding fault, and it will be given to him.

JAMES 1:5

My sister says I'm a selfish pig. She could be right, but what does God want me to do?

Nobody should seek his own good, but the good of others.

1 CORINTHIANS 10:24

Sibling Rivalry

Where is God when my brothers and sisters and I always used to get along, but now all we do is fight?

Rid yourselves of all the offenses you have committed, and get a new heart and a new spirit.

EZEKIEL 18:31

Where is God when my mom just had a baby and I'm jealous that nobody pays attention to me anymore?

Cast your cares on the LORD and he will sustain you; he will never let the righteous fall.

PSALM 55:22

My sister is always taking my clothes without asking. How can I keep her from doing this?

Let us not become weary in doing good, for at the proper time we will reap a harvest if we do not give up.

GALATIANS 6:9

• Vomit.
• Open a bug fogger.
• Hold a sign out the back window: "The driver's an alien; HELP ME!"
• At a stoplight, grab the car keys and throw them out the window.
• Clean the windshield . . . from the outside.
• Bang on the window to see if safety glass is really safe.
• Roll up the windows and scream until their ears turn red.
• Throw your gym socks in the front seat.
• Make faces at law enforcement officers.
• Tell them the truth about your DMV (Department of Motor Vehicles) test scores.
• Light a skyrocket.
• Attempt to be a hood ornament.

(That's all!)

Where is God when I get into a fight with my brother, but I'm the one who always gets punished?

If it is possible, as far as it depends on you, live at peace with everyone.

ROMANS 12:18

Sibling Rivalry

Feeling Unloved

Nobody Loves Me

"'You do not want to leave too, do you?' Jesus asked the Twelve" (John 6:67). Jesus' followers had had enough. Sick and tired of this crazy man claiming to be the Son of God, they split. Miracles? Oh, he had a few tricks up his sleeve, but Jerusalem had as many con men as camels have fleas. *The Son of God? Yeah, right.*

Have you ever wondered if the thought ever crossed Jesus' mind, "Does anybody love me?" Jesus had thousands of followers, but now he was down to just twelve. Lousy stats. Sure he could whip up a fish and bread bash in a flash, but getting the crowds to stay for dessert was tough. He just couldn't hang on to his followers. Did he wonder if anybody really loved him? Did the crowds even hear what he had to say about his Father's love? Would they ever get it?

If you've ever felt as if nobody loves you, then you and Jesus have a lot in common. Jesus knew he was hated. Some people wanted to drop-kick him off a cliff. The crowds picked up rocks to play target practice with his brain. The religious leaders schemed. They plotted. They drew up a death plan. Jesus knows what it's like to feel unloved, but he went to the cross to prove his love for you so you would know that you are loved. "But God demonstrates his own love for us in this: While we were still sinners, Christ died for us" (Rom. 5:8). Next time you're feeling unloved, spend some time with Jesus. Whatever's on your mind, tell him. He's listening. You've got his complete attention. He knows how you feel.

What can I do when I have no one to talk to at home?

I pour out my complaint before him; before him I tell my trouble.

PSALM 142:2

How should I react when my family ignores my problems?

Cast all your anxiety on him because he cares for you.

1 PETER 5:7

Where is God when I was abandoned by my parents as a child and I know I'll never be able to speak with them?

Though my father and mother forsake me, the LORD will receive me.

PSALM 27:10

I'm always home alone after school. Why don't my parents care when I tell them I'm afraid?

Be strong and courageous. Do not be afraid or terrified because of them, for the LORD your God goes with you; he will never leave you nor forsake you.

DEUTERONOMY 31:6

My mom and dad don't seem interested in my life. Has God created me for any purpose?

For we are God's workmanship, created in Christ Jesus to do good works, which God prepared in advance for us to do.

EPHESIANS 2:10

Where can I turn when I can't handle the stress in my home?

When anxiety was great within me, your consolation brought joy to my soul.

PSALM 94:19

Feeling Unloved

Whom can I turn to when I need to be comforted and loved in a way that my family isn't capable of?

Shout for joy, O heavens; rejoice, O earth; burst into song, O mountains! For the LORD comforts his people and will have compassion on his afflicted ones.

ISAIAH **49:13**

My friend has cool parents, and I don't. How can my attitude make the situation bearable?

I know what it is to be in need, and I know what it is to have plenty. I have learned the secret of being content in any and every situation, whether well fed or hungry, whether living in plenty or in want. I can do everything through him who gives me strength.

PHILIPPIANS **4:12–13**

God Provides

Refrigerator Faith

When I was growing up, my family had two refrigerators. One right next to the other. No, we weren't pigs, weight lifters, or grocers. When there are nine people in a family, you either need two refrigerators or one large, restaurant-style refrigerator. My parents probably feared that I'd lock my sisters in the walk-in fridge, so they opted for two smaller, sister-safe refrigerators instead. In my family, we always had food on the table, clothes in the closet, and a roof over our heads. The food was good, the clothes fit, and when my sister was a baby, my dad once found her strolling around naked on the roof of our two-story. That's another story, but all in all, my parents were good providers.

Maybe your needs are being met by your parents. I hope that's true. However, you may come from a home where money is a constant source of frustration. Your mom or dad may be without a job. Firings, layoffs, bankruptcy, bad business deals, and poor decision making can tear families apart quicker than you can say "ATM." Now that I have a family of my own, I have learned this great lesson from Scripture: Not only does God understand financial fears, he promises to provide for our needs. When Jesus' disciples were hanging out with him, they didn't have much money. They didn't know how they were going to make a living. Jesus said to them, "Look at the birds of the air; they do not sow or reap or store away in barns, and yet your heavenly Father feeds them. Are you not much more valuable than they?" (Matt. 6:26). You and your family matter to God. If you are having financial problems, focus your fears on your Provider. He promises to take care of you. Not only are you valuable to him, he has a world full of resources to take care of you. His refrigerator is a lot bigger than his bird feeder.

My mom works two jobs just to make ends meet, but my dad won't get a job. Is he really a Christian?

If anyone does not provide for his relatives, and especially for his immediate family, he has denied the faith and is worse than an unbeliever.

1 TIMOTHY 5:8

My parents say I need to get a job in order to learn discipline with time, money, and work. Why can't I just have fun?

Our people must learn to devote themselves to doing what is good, in order that they may provide for daily necessities and not live unproductive lives.

TITUS 3:14

My family used to be rich, but now we have nothing. Does Jesus understand what it's like to go from having everything to nothing?

For you know the grace of our Lord Jesus Christ, that though he was rich, yet for your sakes he became poor, so that you through his poverty might become rich.

2 CORINTHIANS 8:9

My parents are always giving to charities. Aren't there better things to do with our money?

"Freely you have received, freely give."

MATTHEW 10:8

My dad lost his job. How is God going to help us?

And my God will meet all your needs according to his glorious riches in Christ Jesus.

PHILIPPIANS 4:19

My friends' parents buy them whatever they want. Why won't my parents buy me new clothes when I want them?

"Therefore I tell you, do not worry about your life, what you will eat or drink; or about your body, what you will wear. Is not life more important than food, and the body more important than clothes?"

MATTHEW 6:25

Should I worry about being able to pay our rent at the end of the month?

"Therefore do not worry about tomorrow, for tomorrow will worry about itself. Each day has enough trouble of its own."

MATTHEW 6:34

God Provides

Journal Entry

So What's the Deal with Your Love Life?

_____

_____

_____

_____

_____

_____

_____

_____

_____

_____

_____

_____

_____

So What's the Deal with Your Love Life?

So What's the Deal with Your Love Life?

So What's the Deal with Your Love Life?

So What's the Deal with Your Love Life?

_____

_____

_____

_____

_____

_____

_____

_____

_____

_____

_____

_____

_____

_____

_____

_____

_____

_____

_____

_____

So What's the Deal with Your Love Life?